The New Man

The NEW MAN

An Interpretation of Some Parables and Miracles of Christ

BY
MAURICE NICOLL

SHAMBHALA
Boston & London
1986

Distributed in the United States by Random House and in Canada
by Random House of Canada Ltd.

Printed in the United States of America.

Library of Congress Cataloging in Publication Data

Nicoll, Maurice, 1884–1953.
  The new man.

  Reprint. Originally published: London: Watkins, 1981.
  1. Jesus Christ—Parables. 2. Jesus Christ—Miracles.
I. Title.
BT375.N48 1984   226′.706   83-20279
ISBN 0-87773-268-X (pbk.)
ISBN 0-394-72390-2 (pbk.: Random House)

SHAMBHALA PUBLICATIONS, INC.
314 Dartmouth Street, Boston, MA 02116

CONTENTS

A NOTE ON THE AUTHOR

Dr Maurice Nicoll was born in 1884 in Scotland, the son of Sir William Robertson Nicoll, the well-known littérateur. In his youth he met many famous men at the brilliant gatherings at his father's house in Hampstead, among whom were Lloyd George, Asquith, Sir James Barrie, the young Winston Churchill, and Lord Riddell who frequently refers to conversations at this home in his Diaries.

Dr Nicoll took a first in Science at Caius College, Cambridge, afterwards qualifying in medicine at Bart's Hospital. After studying in Paris, Berlin and Vienna, he entered upon his career as a Harley Street specialist.

In World War I he was a captain in the R.A.M.C. and was in charge of a hospital in Gallipoli. He described his war experiences in a book, In Mesopotamia, published in London in 1917 under the pseudonym of "Martin Swayne".

In 1917 another book came from Dr Nicoll. This was Dream Psychology and in it Dr Nicoll acknowledged his profound debt to Dr Jung with whom he had studied in Zürich.

On his return to Harley Street after the war of 1914–18 Dr Nicoll joined the late Dr George Riddoch at the Empire Hospital, where there were many famous men on the staff. He became a pioneer in psychological medicine and published many papers on medical psychology, from which William McDougall often quoted in his neuro-psychological volumes.

In 1922 Dr Nicoll went for a year to the Institute for the Harmonious Development of Man which G. I. Gurdjieff had established at the Château du Prieuré, Fontainebleau.

Dr Nicoll had met the Russian philosopher P. D. Ouspensky in 1921 who described the teachings and personality of Gurdjieff in the volume, In Search of the Miraculous. Up to 1940 Ouspensky lectured in London. In 1931 he authorised Dr Nicoll to conduct groups for the study of the ideas of Gurdjieff which he continued to do until his death. Dr Nicoll has written a five-volume commentary on the teaching of Gurdjieff and Ouspensky.

Dr Nicoll's leisure activities included building, music, literature and the drama. He painted in oils and water-colour, and the water-colour illustrations in his early book, In Mesopotamia, were his own work.

About his teaching Dr Nicoll said: "Just as we are to-day finding out about all sorts of chemicals, such as the sulphanilamides, penicillin, and streptomycin, so do we have to advance to the study of the poisons of the mind and emotions, the outlines of which further development were laid down in the Gospels."

About his intention in writing The New Man, he said: "The intention is to indicate that all teaching such as that contained in the Gospels, and many teachings both old and new, in the short period of known history, is about transcending the violence which characterises mankind's present level of being. It affirms the possibility of a development of another level of being surmounting violence."

Chapter One

THE LANGUAGE OF PARABLES

PART ONE

ALL sacred writings contain an outer and an inner meaning. Behind the literal words lies another range of meaning, another form of knowledge. According to an old-age tradition, Man once was in touch with this inner knowledge and inner meaning. There are many stories in the Old Testament which convey another knowledge, a meaning quite different from the literal sense of the words. The story of the Ark, the story of Pharaoh's butler and baker, the story of the Tower of Babel, the story of Jacob and Esau and the mess of pottage, and many others, contain an inner *psychological* meaning far removed from their literal level of meaning. And in the Gospels the *parable* is used in a similar way.

Many parables are used in the Gospels. As they stand, taken in the literal meaning of the words, they refer apparently to vineyards, to householders, to stewards, to spendthrift sons, to oil, to water and to wine, to seeds and sowers and soil, and many other things. This is their literal level of meaning. The language of parables is difficult to understand just as is, in general, the language of all sacred writings. Taken on the level of literal understanding, both the Old and New Testaments are full not only of contradictions but of cruel and repulsive meaning.

The question arises: Why are these so-called *sacred* writings cast in misleading form? Why is not what is meant explained clearly? If the story of Jacob's supplanting of Esau, or, again, of the Tower of Babel, or of the Ark constructed in three storeys riding on the flood, is not literally true but has a quite different inner meaning, why is it all not made evident? Why again should *parables* be used in the Gospels? Why not say directly what is meant? And if a person thinking in this way were to ask why the story of Creation in Genesis, which clearly cannot be taken literally, means something else, something quite different from what the literal words mean, he might very well conclude that the so-called sacred writings are nothing but a kind of fraud deliberately perpetrated on

I

Mankind. If all these stories, allegories, myths, comparisons and parables in Sacred Scripture mean something else, why can it not be stated clearly what they mean from the starting-point so that everyone can understand? Why veil everything? Why all this mystery, this obscurity?

The idea behind all sacred writing is to convey a higher meaning than the literal words contain, the truth of which must be seen by Man *internally*. This higher, concealed, inner, or esoteric, meaning, cast in the words and sense-images of ordinary usage, can only be grasped by the understanding, and it is exactly here that the first difficulty lies in conveying higher meaning to Man. A person's literal level of understanding is not necessarily equal to grasping psychological meaning. To understand literally is one thing: to understand psychologically is another. Let us take some examples. The commandment says: "Thou shalt not kill." This is literal. But the psychological meaning is: "Thou shalt not murder in thy heart." The first meaning is literal: the second meaning is psychological, and is actually given in Leviticus. Again the commandment: "Thou shalt not commit adultery" is literal, but the psychological meaning, which is more than this, refers to mixing different doctrines, different teachings. That is why it is often said that people went *whoring* after other gods, and so on. Again, the literal meaning of the commandment: "Thou shalt not steal" is obvious, but the psychological meaning is far deeper. To steal, psychologically, means to think that you do everything *from yourself*, by your own powers, not realising that you do not know who you are or how you think or feel, or how you even move. It is, as it were, taking everything for granted and ascribing everything to yourself. It refers to an attitude. But if a man were told this directly, he would not understand. So the meaning is veiled, because if it were expressed in literal form no one would believe it, and everyone would think it mere nonsense. The idea would not be understood—and worse still, it would be taken as ridiculous. Higher knowledge, higher meaning, if it falls on the ordinary level of understanding, will either seem nonsense, or it will be wrongly understood. It will then become useless, and worse. Higher meaning can only be given to those who are close to grasping it rightly. This is one reason why all sacred writings—that is, writings that are designed to convey more than the literal sense of the words—must be concealed, as it were, by an outer wrapping. It is not a question of misleading people, but a question of preventing this higher meaning from falling in the wrong place, on lower meaning, and thereby having its finer significance destroyed. People sometimes imagine they can understand anything, once they are told it. But this is quite wrong. The development of the understanding, the seeing of differences, is a long process. Everyone knows that little children cannot be taught about life directly because their understanding is small. Again, it is realised that there are subjects in ordinary life that cannot be understood save by long preparation, such as certain branches of the sciences. It is not enough to be merely told what they are about.

The object of all *sacred* writings is to convey higher meaning and higher knowledge in terms of ordinary knowledge as a starting-point. The parables have an ordinary meaning. The object of the *parables* is to give a man higher meaning in terms of lower meaning in such a way that he can either think for himself or not. The parable is an instrument devised for this purpose. It can fall on a man literally, or it can make him think for himself. It invites him to think for himself. A man first understands on his ordinary, matter-of-fact or natural level. To lift the understanding, whatever is taught must first fall on this level to some extent, to form a starting-point. A man must get hold of what he is taught, to begin with, in a natural way. But the parable has meaning beyond its literal or natural sense. It is deliberately designed to fall first on the ordinary level of the mind and yet *to work in the mind* in the direction of lifting the natural level of comprehension to another level of meaning. From this point of view, a parable is a *transforming* instrument in regard to meaning. As we shall see later the parable is also a connecting medium between a lower and a higher level in development of the understanding.

PART TWO

THE Gospels speak mainly of a possible inner evolution called "re-birth". This is their *central* idea. Let us begin by taking inner evolution as meaning a development of the understanding. The Gospels teach that a man living on this earth is capable of undergoing a definite inner evolution if he comes in contact with definite teaching on this subject. For that reason, Christ said: "I am the way, and the truth, and the life" (John xiv, 6). This inner evolution is psychological. To become a more *understanding* person is a psychological development. It lies in the realm of the thoughts, the feelings, the actions, and, in short, the

3

understanding. A man is his understanding. If you wish to see what a man *is*, and not what he is *like*, look at the level of his understanding. The Gospels speak, then, of a *real* psychology based on the teaching that Man on earth is capable of a definite inner evolution in understanding.

The Gospels are from beginning to end all about this possible self-evolution. They are psychological documents. They are about the psychology of this possible inner development—that is, about what a man must think, feel, and do in order to reach a new level of understanding. The Gospels are not about the affairs of life, save indirectly, but about this central idea—namely, that Man internally is a *seed* capable of a definite growth. Man is compared with a seed capable of a definite evolution. As he is, Man is incomplete, unfinished. A man can bring about his own evolution, his own completion, *individually*. If he does not wish to do this he need not. He is then called *grass*—that is, burned up as useless. This is the teaching of the Gospels. But this teaching can be given neither directly nor by external compulsion. A man must begin to *understand for himself* before he can receive it. You cannot make anyone understand by force, by law. But why cannot this teaching be given directly? We come again to the question: "Why cannot higher meaning be given in plain terms? Why all this obscurity? Why these fairy-stories? Why these parables, and so on?" Everyone has an outer side that has been developed by his contact with life and an inner side which remains vague, uncertain, undeveloped. Teaching about re-birth and *inner evolution* must not fall only on the outer side of a man—the life-developed side. Some people reach a stage where they realise that life does not satisfy them, where they genuinely begin to look in other directions and seek different aims, before they can *hear* any teaching of an order similar to that of the Gospels. The outer side of a man is organised by life and its demands, and is according to his position and capacities. In a sense, it is artificial: it is acquired. But it is only the inner, *unorganised* side of a man which can *evolve* as does a seed by its own growth, *from itself*. For that reason the teaching of inner evolution must be so formed that it does not fall solely on the outer side of a man. It must fall there first, but be capable of penetrating more deeply and awakening the man himself—the inner, unorganised man. A man evolves internally through his deeper reflection, not through his outer life-controlled side. He evolves through the spirit of his individual understanding and by inner consent to what he sees as truth. The psycho-

4

logical meaning of the relatively fragmentary teaching recorded in the Gospels refers to this deeper, inner side of everyone. Once one can comprehend that a man can evolve only through a growth in his own individual, and so inner, understanding, one can see that if a true teaching about the meaning of inner evolution falls solely on the outer side of a man it will be useless or will even appear to him as so much nonsense. It may, in fact, be destroyed by falling on the wrong place in him—on his business-side, his worldly side. He will then trample it underfoot. This is the meaning of Christ's remark: "Neither cast your pearls before swine, lest haply they trample them under their feet. . . ." (Matt. vii, 6). "Under" means the outer life-side of a man, the lowest side of a man's understanding, the side which only believes in what his senses shew him, the side of the mind which touches the "earth" as do the feet. This side cannot receive the teaching of inner evolution because it is turned outwards and not inwards. This side therefore cannot understand about re-birth.

A man has one birth, naturally. All esoteric teaching says that he is capable of a second birth. But this re-birth or second birth belongs to the *man in himself*, the private, secret man, the internal man, not to the man as he seems to be in life and thinks himself to be, the successful man, the pretended man. All the latter belongs to the outer man, what the man appears to be, not what the man *is* inwardly. It is the inward man that is the side of re-birth.

In the psychological teaching of the Gospels, a man is not taken as what he appears to be, but as what he most deeply *is*. This is one reason why Christ attacked the Pharisees. For they were *appearances*. They appeared to be good, just, religious, and so on. In attacking the Pharisees, he was attacking that side of a man that pretends, that keeps up appearances for the sake of outer merit, fear, praise, the man who in himself is perhaps even rotten. The Pharisee, psychologically understood, is the outer side of a man who pretends to be good, virtuous, and so on. It is that side of yourself. This is the Pharisee in every man and this is the psychological meaning of Pharisee. Everything said in the Gospels, whether represented in the form of parable, miracle or discourse, has a *psychological* meaning, apart from the literal sense of the words. Therefore the psychological meaning of the *Pharisees* refers, not to certain people who lived long ago, but to oneself now— *to the Pharisee in oneself*, to the insincere person in oneself, who, of course, cannot receive any real and genuine psychological teaching without turning it into an

5

occasion for merit, praise and award. Later on we will study the meaning of the *Pharisee in oneself* more fully.

PART THREE

SINCE all sacred writings contain both a literal and a psychological meaning they can fall in a double way on the mind. If Man were capable of no further development this would have no sense. It is just because he is capable of a further individual evolution that parables exist. The "sacred" idea of Man—that is, the esoteric or inner idea—is that he possesses an unused higher level of understanding and that his real development consists in reaching this higher possible level. So all sacred writings, as in the form of parables, have a double meaning because they contain a literal meaning designed to fall on the level of a man as he is, and at the same time they can reach up to the higher level potentially present in him and awaiting him.

A parable is cast in the form of *ancient meaning*. A parable in the Gospels is cast in the form of an ancient language now forgotten. There was a time when the language of parables could be understood. This language—the language of the parable, allegory and miracle—is lost to the humanity of to-day. But sources still remain which enable us to understand something of this ancient meaning. Since the object of the parable is to connect higher and lower meanings, it can be thought of as a *bridge* between two levels, a *liaison* between literal and psychological understanding. And, as we shall see, a definite language was once well known, in which this *double rendering* was understood and certain words and terms deliberately used in an understood double sense. Through this ancient language a connexion was made between higher and lower meaning—or, which is the same—the higher and lower sides of man.

Our first birth is from the world of cells by evolution into that of Man. To be re-born or born again means to evolve up to a higher psychology, a higher possible level of understanding. This is Man's supreme aim, according to the teaching of all ancient Scriptures in which Man is regarded psychologically as an undeveloped seed. And this is esoteric teaching. This level can only be reached by new knowledge and the feeling and practice of it; and the knowledge that

6

gives a man this possibility is sometimes called, in the Gospels, Truth, or some-times the *Word*. But it is not ordinary truth, or ordinary knowledge. It is know-ledge about this further step in development.

Let us try to gain some preliminary ideas about this ancient double language of parables. Let us begin by studying how Truth is represented. In this ancient language visible things represent psychological things. Outer life, registered by the senses, is transformed into another level of meaning.

Now Truth is not a visible object, but it was represented by means of a visible object in this language. A parable is full of visible imagery of the objects of the senses. But each visual image represents something belonging to a psychological level of meaning, distinct from the image used. In the Gospels the word *water* is often used. What does this word mean in the ancient language? In the literal sense of the word it means the physical substance called water. But psychologic-ally, on a higher level of meaning, it has a different import. Water does not mean simply water. Christ, in speaking of re-birth to Nicodemus, says that a man must be born of *water* and the spirit: "Except a man be born of *water* and the spirit, he cannot enter into the kingdom of God" (John iii, 5). What then does water mean? It must have another meaning, a psychological or higher meaning. We might guess, perhaps, that the "spirit" means possibly the "will" or the inmost, most real part of a man. And we might understand that to be born again does not mean literally to enter the womb of the mother again, as Nicodemus thought, who stands for a man capable only of literal understanding. Whatever we may think about the meaning of "spirit", we cannot imagine, with our ordinary comprehension, what "water" means in this ancient double-sided language, in which things of the senses convey another and special meaning. There is no clue. To say that a man must be born again of physical water is sheer nonsense. What then does water mean psychologically? We can find, by means of other passages in the Bible, what this physical image represents on the psycho-logical level of meaning. A hundred examples might be quoted. Let us take one from the Gospels. Christ spoke to the Woman of Samaria by the well-side and told her he could give her "living water". Christ says to her when she has come to draw water at the well:

"Everyone that drinketh of this water shall thirst again: but whosoever drinketh of the water that I shall give him shall never thirst; but the water that I shall give him shall become in him a well of water springing up into eternal life."

(John iv, 13–14.)

It is plain that "water" is being used in a special sense, belonging to this ancient forgotten language. Again in the Old Testament, in the Book of Jeremiah, it is said:

"For my people have committed two evils; they have forsaken me the fountain of living waters, and hewed them out cisterns, broken cisterns, that can hold no water."

(Jeremiah ii, 13.)

What then is this water, this *living water*?

In the ancient language *water* means Truth. But it means a special kind of Truth, a special form of knowledge called "living Truth". It is living Truth because it makes a man *alive in himself*, and not dead, once the knowledge of it is assented to and applied in practice. In esoteric teaching—that is, teaching about inner evolution—a man is called *dead* who knows nothing about it. It is knowledge that is true only in reference to the reaching of this higher level of inner evolution awaiting everyone. It is knowledge about this higher level of Man and leading to it. It refers to what a man must know, think, feel, understand and do to reach his next stage of development. It is not outer truth, about outer things, outer objects, but inner Truth, about the man himself and the kind of person he is and how he can change himself. It is therefore *esoteric* Truth (esoteric meaning inner) or Truth referring to that inner development and new organisation of a man that leads to his next step in real evolution. For no one can change, no one can become different, no one can evolve and reach this higher possible level and so be re-born, unless he knows, hears and follows a teaching about it. If he thinks he knows Truth of this order by himself then he is like those mentioned above who "forsake the living waters and hew out for themselves cisterns, broken cisterns, that can hold no water". The idea is quite plain. A teaching exists—and has always existed—that can lead to a higher development. This teaching is the real psychological teaching in regard to Man and the possible development of the New Man in him. Man cannot invent it by himself. He can hew out cisterns for himself but they hold no water—that is, no Truth.

8

THE LANGUAGE OF PARABLES

When there is no Truth of this order the state of Man is sometimes compared with thirst.

"The poor and needy seek water and there is none, and their tongue faileth for thirst;"   (Isaiah xli, 17.)

Or when people follow wrong truth a comparison is sometimes made with drinking bitter waters, or with undrinkable or polluted water.

Let us now apply this idea of water meaning Truth, in this ancient language, to one of the sayings of Christ, and realise what psychological meaning is, in contrast to literal meaning. Christ said:

"And whosoever shall give to drink unto one of these little ones a cup of cold water only, in the name of a disciple, verily I say unto you, he shall in no wise lose his reward."   (Matt. x, 42.)

Here a literal-minded person will think that all that is necessary is to give a cup of cold water to a child. But if water means Truth, then the phrase refers to the handing on of Truth, however poorly. And "little one" here does not mean a child (in the Greek) but a person small in understanding. Let us also notice that, to receive Truth, the mind must be like a cup, which receives what is poured into it. That is, a man must be ready and willing to be taught, so that his mind is like a cup to receive water. So the phrase "giving a cup of water" refers both to receiving Truth and handing it on to others.

All this cannot be logically expressed, but it can be psychologically understood. And this is exactly the intention of the ancient language we have begun to study.

PART FOUR

OTHER words for Truth are used in the esoteric writings of the Old and New Testaments. *Water* is not the only image used to represent the order of Truth that we are studying. In the ancient language *stone* and *wine* are both used as images for this form of Truth, but on different scales of meaning.

Stone represents the most external and literal form of esoteric Truth. It represents esoteric Truth in its most inflexible sense. The commandments were written

9

on tables of *stone*. It must be understood that Truth about a higher evolution must rest upon a firm basis, for those incapable of seeing any deeper meaning.

Let us take briefly the extraordinary story of the Tower of Babel recorded in Genesis. The ideas centred in this story refer to Man trying by his ordinary knowledge to reach a higher level of development. This is the meaning of the tower that was built by Man. But from what has been said so far it can be realised that to reach a higher level for a man personally or for Mankind, the teaching of the knowledge necessary for this further step must be known and be followed. Man cannot add to his stature "by taking thought"—that is, his own ideas, his own thoughts, cannot bring him up to a new level of evolution. He must submit to a teaching. His efforts must be based on this Truth that we are studying. And this special knowledge or esoteric Truth, at its lowest level of comprehending, is called *stone*. We shall see what the Tower of Babel was built of, in regard to this necessary knowledge called Truth. It was not *stone*, and it is expressly said that it was not so. That is, it did not come from a higher level of Man—from those who have become New Men.

The story of the Tower of Babel is very strange and has little meaning if we take it literally. It begins by saying that once upon a time, after the days of Noah and the Ark, all people had a common language. "And the whole earth was of one language and one speech" (Genesis xi, 1). Then it is said that they journeyed "from the east" (i.e. away from Truth) and came to a plain, and began to think of building a tower to reach to heaven. Notice how the account continues: "And they had brick for stone and slime they had for mortar. And they said, Go to, let us build us a city, and a tower, whose top may reach unto heaven, and let us make us a name. . . ." Notice that they travelled from the east and they had brick—a man-made thing—and not stone. The east represents, in the ancient language of parables, the source of esoteric Truth. They reached a plain—that is, came down from a higher level—and then began to think that they could of themselves *do* something, apart from what knowledge of Truth they had gained "from the east". So they began to build a tower—that is, they thought that they could, out of their own ideas and thoughts, reach to the highest level, here called "heaven" and also called similarly in the Gospel language. "Heaven" means a higher level of Man and "earth" means an ordinary man—the natural man.

They began to build for themselves, but notice that it is expressly said that they not only had bricks for *stone*, but *slime* for mortar.

A higher level cannot be understood by a lower level. A man on a higher level cannot be understood by a man on a lower level. Man as he is cannot reach a higher level unless he comes into possession of the knowledge (called Truth) that can lead him to it. So the Tower was a failure. And in the strange way in which this ancient language puts things, it looks as if "God" scattered them out of jealousy. But one must look deeper to understand this language. Man was at fault, not "God". Man tried to raise himself by his own knowledge, called here "brick" and "slime"—and so was shattered.

"And the whole earth was of one language and of one speech. And it came to pass, as they journeyed from the east, that they found a plain in the land of Shinar; and they dwelt there. And they said one to another, Go to, let us make brick, and burn them throughly. And they had brick for stone, and slime they had for mortar. And they said, Go to, let us build us a city and a tower, whose top may reach unto heaven; and let us make us a name, lest we be scattered abroad upon the face of the whole earth. And the Lord came down to see the city and the tower, which the children of men builded. And the Lord said, Behold, the people is one, and they have all one language; and this they begin to do: and now nothing will be restrained from them, which they have imagined to do. Go to, let us go down and there confound their language, that they may not understand one another's speech. So the Lord scattered them abroad from thence upon the face of all the earth: and they left off to build the city. Therefore is the name of it called Babel; because the Lord did there confound the language of all the earth: and from thence did the Lord scatter them abroad upon the face of all the earth."   (Genesis xi, 1–9.)

But it is very difficult to understand the ancient language if we take it literally. We can understand that if an engineer makes some part of an engine that is wrongly measured or of the wrong material, his engine will be no good. He may say: "It is God's fault". It is not "God" punishing: it is a wrong "request" and so the response will not be as he hoped. The response will be according to the quality of his request. And this is "God" or, if you like, the "Universe", that science studies. A wrong request leads to a wrong response. It is not really a wrong response but an exactly right response in view of the request. The parable of the Tower of Babel is an illustration of this. Man made a tower out of brick and slime, in place of *stone* and mortar. And "God" said—that is, response to request said: "this cannot be", in so many words.

Now let us look at other examples of *stone* as a term meaning, in the ancient language, Truth about a higher development. To reach a higher state of himself a man must request rightly and for this to come about a man must *know* what to ask for. Christ says: "Ask and ye shall receive." But unless we know something about either the *stone* or the *water* of esoteric knowledge, how can we know what to ask for? Christ is not speaking about asking for life-things, but about asking for help in inner evolution and understanding. Certain requests are made in the Lord's Prayer. They are about *right asking*. But we will study this later. Now let us take the strange incident of Christ's re-naming Simon. *Simon* means "a hearing", but Christ re-named Simon *Peter*, which in the Greek is *stone*. Christ, of course, represents this Truth of which we are speaking. He called himself "the Truth". He spoke of a high level of evolution for each individual man. He taught the means of attaining it. He taught *re-birth*. Now in re-naming Simon as Peter, he referred to the literal aspect of his teaching. Christ said to Simon: "Thou art Peter, and upon this stone I will build my church; and the gates of Hades shall not prevail against it. I will give unto thee the keys of the kingdom of heaven . . ." (Matt. xvi, 18–19). Simon Peter was given the "keys of the kingdom of heaven". Heaven means psychologically this higher level of development, intrinsically possible for man. But Christ only gave Peter, as the *stone*, the keys. The commandments, written on stone, are keys also. But, literally taken, they are not enough. They open into psychological meaning. They contain great internal meaning. Esoteric Truth in the form of *stone* is not flexible enough to lead to any real inner development. It must be *understood*, not merely followed blindly. In Genesis it is said that Jacob rolled away the stone from the well. The stone in the mouth of the well means in the ancient language that literal Truth blocks the psychological understanding of it. The stone was rolled back and the flock *watered*: for *water* is the psychological understanding of literal esoteric Truth called *stone*. In this way can the following passage be understood:

"Then Jacob went on his journey, and came to the land of the children of the east. And he looked, and behold, a well in the field, and lo, three flocks of sheep lying there by it; for out of that well they watered the flocks: and the stone upon the well's mouth was great. And thither were all the flocks gathered: and they rolled the stone from the well's mouth, and watered the sheep."

(Genesis xxix, 1–3.)

When a stone blocks the well, it means that people have taken esoteric Truth literally, in the sense of the words only. They prefer rituals and so on. They literally "do not kill" but see no reason why they should not murder in their hearts.

Christ himself, who represented esoteric Truth or "the Way" or the "Word", was called "the stone which the builders rejected". The Psalmist says: "The stone which the builders rejected is become the head of the corner." (Ps. 118, 22.) This is a strange phrase. Who are the builders? The builders of what? Of this world? Certainly Christ's teaching came into a world built of violence, a world in which everyone believed that violence leads to something better. But when Christ is called the *stone* it means that fundamentally he was so. His whole teaching, however, was to transform stone into water and finally water into wine. The Jews understood everything literally, as stone. Christ transformed literal into psychological meaning. This is shewn in one of the "miracles", which are really psychological miracles—that is, the transformation of literal meaning into psychological understanding. A man who is bound down to the literal meaning of higher truth can destroy himself. This explains, perhaps, why some religious people seem to be destroyed by their contact with religion and made worse than life would make them. This is possibly shewn in the account in the fifth chapter of Mark of the man with an unclean spirit who came out of the tombs, of whom it is said that he was always "cutting himself with stones". *Stones*—that is, taking higher Truth at a literal level—cut him, made him unclean. And since Jesus represented, let us say at present, a higher understanding of literal Truth, the man cried out to him: "What have I to do with thee, Jesus?" And Jesus said: "Come forth, thou unclean spirit, out of the *man*." The *man* means the man's understanding which is the real man. But this is only a slight glimpse of the meaning of this miracle-parable. It refers to a certain state of a man in regard to higher teaching. The point here is that the man "cut himself with *stones*"—that is, took higher truth literally and was therefore *unclean*. And his uncleanness had to pass

13

into the swine. But perhaps we shall be able to understand something more of what this means later on.

Jesus always represents the non-literal or non-ritualistic understanding of higher Truth. The Jews in the Gospels *represent* not actual, literal people, but a certain literal level of taking everything belonging to higher Truth. Everyone is a *Jew* who cannot get from the sense of the letter to the psychological meaning. So the Jews are said to "stone Christ". When Christ said: "I and the Father are one" it is said that "The Jews took up stones again to stone him," because their literal minds thought his words were blasphemy. The inner meaning is that people on the level of literal and so ritualistic, external understanding throw this meaning at people who stand above its level. One can even be *stoned* by what one once understood in a literal way and now understands quite differently. And one can always *stone* a man through his actual, literal words, without allowing any existence to what he really *meant*. And literal law, of the legal courts, is and must be based on *stone*—that is, on what you actually said in words and not on what you meant.

PART FIVE

LET us speak for a moment about *wine* used as an image for Truth. We shall study the meaning of esoteric Truth when it has reached the stage of wine in a man's understanding later. But at present we must understand that *stone* is the literal form of esoteric Truth, and *water* refers to another way of understanding the same Truth, and *wine* to the highest form of understanding it. In the miracle recorded in the second chapter of St John's Gospel, Christ turned water into wine. In this account it is said that he asked the servants to fill the *stone*-jars with *water* and then he transformed the water into *wine*. That is, three stages of a man's relation to Truth are shewn, and this means, of course, three stages in the understanding of esoteric Truth.

PART SIX

THE idea of wine leads naturally to the idea of *vineyards* which produce wine. Before we can continue more fully the study of the ancient language of parables, we must look at the meaning of *vineyards* and try to get some idea of their significance. It will be necessary to speak further of this Truth that refers to a man's inner development and growth of understanding. This Truth is not ordinary truth. It is sown on the earth. For example, Christ taught this particular kind of Truth. In the Sermon on the Mount he spoke quite openly about certain aspects of it. But the deeper aspects of it he concealed under the guise of parables.

Man cannot invent this Truth for himself. We have seen that this is indicated in the story of the Tower of Babel where men thought they could reach Heaven by means of "brick and slime" instead of stone and mortar. Higher Truth, which simply means Truth that leads to a higher level of self-evolution, does not arise in life, but comes from those who have already reached this higher level. Many have reached it. Some few of them are recorded in ordinary history. Let us confine ourselves to Christ. He taught this higher Truth. But he spoke many things about the establishment of this special order of Truth on earth and used the image of a *vineyard*. A school of teaching, based on Truth of this order, was called by him a vineyard, and its object was to produce fruit. If it did not, it was cut down. Christ also speaks of himself as a vine and he says to his disciples:

"I am the vine, ye are the branches: he that abideth in me, and I in him, the same beareth much fruit: for apart from me ye can do nothing."

(John xv, 5.)

Christ relates the following parable about a vineyard:

"A certain man had a fig-tree planted in his vineyard; and he came seeking fruit thereon, and found none. And he said unto the vinedresser, Behold, these three years I come seeking fruit on this fig-tree, and find none: cut it down: why doth it also cumber the ground? And he answering saith unto him, Lord, let it alone this year also, till I shall dig about it, and dung it; and if it bear fruit thenceforth, well; but if not, thou shalt cut it down."   (Luke xiii, 6–9.)

From this point of view Man was regarded as capable of a special growth, a special inner development, and "vineyards" were established to make this development possible. Of course, they were not actual vineyards. They were *schools* of teaching. What did they teach? They taught, first of all, the knowledge that could

15

lead, *if practised,* to the higher level of development inherent in Man. What they taught a man was that he was an individual—that is, unique—who could reach this higher state of himself and that this was his real meaning and that this only could satisfy him most deeply. They began with teaching this Truth—or knowledge of this special Truth—but they led to something else. They led from Truth to a definite state of a man where he acted no longer from the Truth that brought him up to this level, but from the level itself. This was sometimes called *Good. All Truth must lead to some good state as its goal.* This was the idea belonging to the term "vineyard". Wine was produced. A man began to act from Good, not Truth, thus becoming a New Man.

from principles/teachings/beliefs about...
to ACTION from within that reality

from Truth, relative, to GOOD

Chapter Two

THE IDEA OF TEMPTATION IN THE GOSPELS

PART ONE

A S we shall study in the next chapter the Miracle of the Transformation of Water into Wine, which in its internal or psychological meaning is about a certain definite stage reached by Jesus in his individual evolution, approximately just before he began to teach, it may be as well to consider the temptations of Jesus and the idea of temptation in its general significance in the Gospels in this connexion. Now here it is necessary to grasp clearly something that is not usually understood. What has to be grasped is that *Jesus had to undergo inner growth and evolution.* He was not born perfect. Had this been the case he would not have suffered temptation or experienced such despair. Some religious people make a mistake in thinking that Christ had from the start such exceptional powers that anything was possible to him. But, as one instance, Jesus mentions the difficulty of healing a certain form of illness and says that much prayer and fasting is necessary before it can be undertaken. Later on we shall study some of these examples, but it can be said here that the most extraordinary views exist about the unlimited powers that Jesus had on earth, so much so that people even argue that if he were the Son of God, why did he not heal all sickness and convert the whole world? This is the same kind of argument used by people who say that if there is a God why are pain, illness, suffering, war, and so on, allowed on earth? The whole standpoint of both arguments is wrong. The idea of the meaning of life on earth is not grasped. In fact, the central idea of the Gospels is not grasped—namely, the idea of individual evolution and re-birth.

* * *

Let us repeat the words used above to make the issue of this chapter as clear as possible: *Jesus had to undergo inner growth and evolution.* Let us start from this point. Jesus was not born perfect, as a fully-developed, a fully-evolved Man. On

17

the contrary, he was born imperfect in order to carry out a certain long-prophesied task. He had to re-establish at a critical period in human history a connexion between the two levels called in the Gospels "earth" and "heaven", and this had to be done in himself *practically*, so as to reopen a way for influences from a higher level of the Universe of Total Being (which extends up through different degrees of the Divine Being to Absolute Being) to reach Mankind on earth and so make it possible for Man to have a possibility of inner development and also for some kind of intelligent culture to exist for a definite period or cycle of history. Of this period Jesus asks himself whether "faith will be found on earth" at its culmination. "Howbeit when the Son of Man cometh, shall he find faith on earth?" Such are the words of Christ and these words suggest that he doubted whether faith would be found on earth at the end of this cycle.

Jesus then had to bridge the human and divine in himself and in this way re-establish a connexion between heaven and earth. He had to undergo all the difficulties of an inner evolution of the *human in him* so that it became subject to the higher or "divine" level. He had to pass through all the stages of this evolution *in himself* by trial and error, until it was perfected, through endless inner tempt-ations, of which we are only given a few glimpses. And all this took place over a long period about which we only know something of the teaching he gave during the latter part of it, which terminated in the final humiliation and so-called catastrophe of the crucifixion, and a few details of the earliest part, but nothing of the comparatively long, intervening part. Here is silence. We do not know where Jesus was taught during this period or by whom he was given directions for the final drama he had to enact, the heralding of which was given to John the Baptist (who did not know him by sight) and the ordained culmination of which is referred to by Jesus in many places, and, in the Miracle of the Transformation of Water into Wine, in the words he is made to say to his mother: "Mine hour is not yet come". (He does not say "mother", but *woman*.) Yet some religious people imagine that Jesus was crucified because of Pilate—as it were, by chance. This view is absurd. He had to play the part allotted to him. It was pre-arranged.

Now in the earliest references to the development of Jesus it is said that he *advanced* in wisdom and stature. Jesus advanced by stages. In Luke it is said: "The child grew and waxed strong in spirit and was filled with wisdom, and grace was upon him" (Luke ii, 52). Luke—who never saw Jesus—also records his first words when he was found in the Temple at the age of twelve by his father and mother after a search of three days. His mother is made to say: "Son, why have you treated us like this? Do you know, your father and I have sought you sorrowing?" To which Jesus is made to answer: "How is it that ye sought me? Do you not know that I must be in all that belongs to my Father?" Notice that the distinction between "father on earth" and "Father in Heaven" is made—that is, between the idea of the first earthly birth and the second higher birth which was the subject of Christ's teaching. Even at the age of twelve those who listened to him in the Temple were "amazed at his understanding and his answers". The idea, then, of Jesus *advancing* in understanding is quite distinct. And it is clear that a long period elapsed before he had advanced to his full inner stature and attained his supreme development, called in the Gospels the moment of his *glorification*. This final fulfilment of his evolution began when Judas went out into the night to "betray" him, as it is called, and when Jesus said to his remaining disciples: "Now is the Son of Man glorified". But even then, it was not yet attained for he obviously had to undergo two further and very severe temptations—the temptation in Gethsemane where he prayed: "O my Father, if it be possible, let this cup pass away from me: nevertheless not as I will but as thou wilt," and the temptation on the Cross where he cried out: "My God, why hast thou forsaken me?" Here must also be remarked that Christ began to teach some three years before he attained glorification—that is, before his full development.

Let us ask ourselves: How is inner evolution reached? All inner development is possible only through inner temptation. Three temptations of Christ by the devil are mentioned in detail in the early parts of the Gospels of Matthew and Luke, and referred to very briefly in Mark, in terms of "wild beasts". Nothing is said of this in John but the Miracle of Water into Wine is made as the starting-point of the teaching and miracles of Jesus. Let us study for the present the version of the three early temptations as given in Luke, in order to realise that Jesus had to advance by undergoing development by the method of temptation and so pass through *stages of inner growth*, by means of inner self-conquest. But let us first remember that the conception of Mankind in its unawakened state as given in the Gospels is that it is in the power of evil and this is represented by the idea that Man is infested by evil spirits. That is, Man is under the power of evil moods and impulses and thoughts, which are personified as evil spirits, whose object is the destruction of a man and of the human race. The conception of the Gospels is that Man is continually being dragged down by evil forces, *which are in him*, not outside him, and to which he consents. By Man's consent to these forces *in himself*, progress in human life is prevented. The evil powers are in Man, in his own nature, in the very nature of his self-love, his egotism, his ignorance, his stupidity, his malice, his vanity, and also his thinking only from the senses and taking the seen world, the outer appearances of life, as the only reality. These defects are collectively called the *devil*, which is the name for the *terrible power of misunderstanding everything* that undeveloped Man possesses, the power of *wrongly connecting* everything. The devil is the aggregate of all these deficiencies, all these *powers of misunderstanding in Man*, and all their transmitted results. So the devil is called the *slanderer* or scandal-maker, from one point of view, and the *accuser* from another point of view. But we shall see a little more clearly what is meant by the devil when we begin to understand what temptation really means.

In the account of the tempting of Christ by the devil given in Luke, it is said that Jesus was in the wilderness for forty days, "being tempted of the devil". This number *forty* appears in the account of the Flood, where the rain lasted for *forty* days and nights, in the allegorical account of the Children of Israel wandering *forty* years in the wilderness, and it is said also of Moses that he fasted *forty* days and nights before he received the Commandments written on tablets of *stone*. Here, in Luke, the *forty* days in the wilderness are directly connected with the *idea of temptation*:

"Jesus was led by the Spirit in the wilderness during forty days, being tempted by the devil. And he did eat nothing in those days and when they were completed he hungered." (Luke iv, 1-2.)

Then comes a description of the first resulting temptation of this period of temptation, which is represented in the following way:

"And the devil said unto him, If thou art the Son of God command this stone that it becomes a loaf of bread." (Luke iv, 3.)

Let us take the superficial literal or first level of meaning. Christ hungered and the devil suggests that he should transform a stone into bread.

"And Jesus answered and said unto him, It is written, man shall not live by bread alone." (Luke iv, 4.)

On the literal level this is just as it appears—a physical temptation. Notice, however, that it is said above that Jesus was in the wilderness forty days "being tempted of the devil". If we suppose the wilderness to be a literal physical wilderness, how is it that nothing is said about how he was being tempted all this time? One might merely say that he was starving. But in connexion with inner development we must understand by the term *wilderness* a state of mind, a general inner state, comparable with a literal wilderness—that is, a state where there is nothing to guide a man, where he is no longer among familiar things and so is in a wilderness, a state of distress and bewilderment and perplexity, where he is left entirely to himself, as a test, and does not know in which direction to go and must not go in his own direction. This itself is temptation, for all the time he is being starved of meaning. Why should a man leave the familiar and go into a wilderness? He hungers for bread—not literal bread but that bread that we ask for in the Lord's Prayer, so wrongly translated as "daily" bread—namely, guidance, trans-substantial bread, and, literally, bread for the *to-morrow*, in fact, meaning, for the development of our lives, not for our lives as they are to-day, now, but as they can become, the bread necessary for our support in growing, the bread for successive and necessary stages of *understanding*. (For the Lord's Prayer is a prayer about inner evolution and the bread asked for is the bread of understanding necessary for it.) In such a state the temptation is *to make bread for oneself*—that is, to follow one's own ideas, one's own will—exactly as the builders of the "Tower of Babel" used bricks and slime of their own making, in place of stone and mortar. They thought they could make a new world from their own ideas. Why should one not fall back on oneself and so on life once more instead of waiting for something that seems doubtful? In Matthew the answer of Christ to this temptation is:

"Man shall not live by bread alone, but by every word that proceedeth out of the mouth of God." (Matt. iv, 4.)

See clearly that the devil has asked Christ to make *bread by himself* to ease his state—that is, not to await the Word of God. The devil says: "If thou art the Son of God, command that these stones become bread." That is, nourish yourself by your own powers and ideas. But the mission of Christ, which began immediately after the temptations in the wilderness, was not to manufacture truth and meaning by himself, but to understand and teach the Truth and meaning of the Word of God—that is, of a higher level of influences. The test was as to his own self-will and the will of a higher level. He had to do the will of "God"—not his own will. He had to bring the lower human level in himself under subjection to the will of the higher or divine level. It is the human level here that is under temptation for Jesus was born of a human mother. To mistake the lower for the higher is the annihilation of a man, for then he will ascribe to himself what does not belong to him. A man will then be tempted to say: "I am God", and not "God is I". If he says: "I am God", he identifies himself with God *from a lower level*. This annihilates him. If he says: "God is I", he surrenders his self-will and makes the will of God "I" in him and so is under, and must obey, God—that is, a higher level. Notice that the devil is made to address Jesus in the words: "If thou art the Son of God . . ." and so suggests that Jesus can do as he likes, as if he were at the level of God. All this was in Jesus. It took place *in him*. And although this temptation can be taken quite simply as one relative to overcoming the appetites, in this case, hunger, it is clear that other and far deeper meanings lie behind the literal meaning and that they are concerned with those problems of self-love and power—and violence—in which human nature is rooted. Jesus had *human nature* in him from the woman—his mother. The task was to transform it. This is quite obvious in the second temptation, where Christ is offered all power over the visible world. The devil is represented as leading Christ to a "high place" and shewing him all the kingdoms of the world *in a point of time:*

"He led him up, and shewed him all the kingdoms of the world in a moment of time. And the devil said unto him, To thee will I give all this authority, and the glory of them: for it hath been delivered unto me; and to whomsoever I will I give it. If thou therefore wilt worship before me, it shall be thine." (Luke iv, 5-7.)

This is temptation as to earthly power and the deep vanity that lies in everyone. It is again directed to the self-love. It includes love of the world and its possessions. The devil will give Christ the world. Love of power (authority) and

22

love of possessions represent two sides of self-love. Here the human level in Christ is represented as being subject to the most tremendous temptation conceivable in regard to worldy gain and possessive power. The temptation is described in such a way as to bring this out clearly: the whole world is presented to Jesus "in a point of time"—that is, simultaneously. Jesus is made to answer: "It is written, Thou shalt worship the Lord thy God and him only shalt thou serve." That is, not the world and its possessions. The answer is from the same ground of understanding as that given in the first temptation. There is something apart from the world and the love of possessing it. There is something else that Man must possess. This higher level, both possible to Man and already in a man, is the direction in which his desire for power and glory must turn. But even although a man *knows* and is quite certain about this direction, he can still be tempted—and even more so. Otherwise Christ would not have been tempted in this way. His human side was still open to this temptation. It is not only the overwhelming effect of the senses and any immediate appeal to self-interest and vanity that has to be thought of here but perhaps the far subtler ideas of being able, by worldy means and outer power and authority, to help mankind by becoming *a king on earth.*We know that the disciples thought Jesus was going to be an *earthly king* possessing the whole world and give them earthly rewards. They thought from the lower level about higher things. They could not at first see what Jesus was talking about—namely, the reaching of a higher or inner level which has nothing to do with the lower or outer level of life.We must remember here that the path that Christ had to follow led to apparent failure in outer life, and outer powerlessness—and to a death reserved only for the worst criminals. He had only a few ultimate followers. It looked as if everything had been useless. Certainly we cannot expect to understand this unless we grasp the whole idea of two levels. But we shall speak more of this later on, and only say here that temptation in the real sense is about these two levels and relates to the passage from one to the other. If Jesus had been born perfect, he would have been beyond all temptation. He would not have represented the *New Man* or the Way to it. He called himself the *Way*: "I am the Way", for this reason.

PART TWO

THERE are different ways in which we can be tempted and different ways in which we can yield to temptation. Let us speak of temptation in general. All temptation (if it is real) implies a struggle between two things in a man, each of which aims at getting control. This struggle has two forms. It is always either between what is true and what is false, or between what is good and what is bad. The whole inner drama of Man's life and the result of it all, in terms of his inner development, lie in this inner struggle about what is the Truth and what is a lie, and what is good and what is bad. And actually it is about these things that everyone is always thinking and wondering in the privacy of his mind and heart. The mind is for thinking what is true and the heart for perceiving what is good.

Let us take first temptation in regard to Truth. This takes place in the intellectual life of a person. Everyone holds to certain things he regards as true. Knowledge itself is not Truth, for we know many things but do not regard all of them as necessarily true, or we are indifferent to them. But out of all the things we know, some we hold to be true. This is our personal Truth, and it belongs to our personal, intellectual life, for knowledge and Truth are of the mind. Now the intellectual life of a man is nothing but what he believes to be true and when this is assailed in any way, he feels anxiety. The more he values what he believes to be true the more anxiety will he feel when doubt enters his mind. This is a mild state of temptation, in which a man must think about what he believes and values as Truth and from it fight with his doubts. You must understand that no one can be tempted about what he does not value. It is only in connexion with what he values that he can be tempted. The meaning of temptation is to strengthen all that a man values as Truth. Throughout the Gospels the idea that a man must struggle and fight in himself is apparent. The Gospels are about the inner development and evolution of a man. This demands inner struggle— that is, temptation is necessary. But people are sometimes offended at the idea that they must fight for Truth, and must go through temptations in regard to it. But it is necessary to fight for knowledge as much as to fight with oneself.

Now let us take temptation in regard to Good. This is not intellectual but emotional. It belongs to the side that a man wills, not what he thinks. The basis of what a man wills is what he feels is good. Everyone wills and acts from what he feels is good, and all that a man wills belongs to his voluntary life. Nothing else makes the voluntary life of a man but that which he has impressed upon himself as being good. If all that a man holds as Good were taken away from him, his voluntary life would cease, just as if all that a man believes to be Truth were taken away from him, his intellectual life would cease. Now in the Gospels all Truth has to do with knowledge of the teaching given by Christ, and all Good has to do with the love of God and the love of one's neighbour. Now whatever a man loves he regards as good, and what he regards as good he wills and acts from. If he only loves himself then he is a man to whom Good means only his own good, and anything that does not apply to his own good he will regard as bad. The development of the will is through the development of the love, and the development of the love is at the expense of the self-love. Now since a man can only be tempted intellectually through what he values as Truth, he can only be tempted in regard to his will and deeds through what he loves. And since all temptation in a real sense is about the Truth of the Word—that is, the teaching of the Gospels—and the Good of the Word, temptation as to Good as distinct from Truth only begins when a man begins to pass beyond the level of self-love into what is called *charity* or love of neighbour through a sense of the existence of God as the source of love. Temptations as to Truth necessarily begin long before temptations as to Good, but if there is no sort of natural charity in a man, his temptations as to Truth will be less easy to pass through. Truth must enter and grow in a man first before he can change the direction of his will—that is, before his feeling of what is good can change. When he begins to feel the feeling of new Good entering him the two feelings will *alternate*. Later he will feel a struggle between the new Good and what he formerly felt as good. But by this time he should be able to hold on to Truth, however he fails in regard to Good. The man is really between two *levels*, lower and upper, and all real temptation only begins when this is the case, for the lower level attracts him and he has to find a path between them. Actually he lifts himself up a little and falls back like a drunken man trying to get off the floor. But if temptation as to Good really begins, whatever it results in, at any time, he must never let failure or apparent failure war against the Truth on to which he is holding. If he does, he will lose some sense of Truth with each failure. Whatever he is or does, he must hold to the Truth he has received and keep it alive in him.

In the third temptation of Christ, the devil once more begins by saying: "If thou art the Son of God. . . ." We must understand that Christ had to fight against self-love in all its forms and all kinds of earthly loves and everything derived from them. He had to overcome every feeling of self-power arising from the human level in him so as to make it subject to the higher level. Now temptation in a real sense has to do with the relation of the lower level in a man to any higher possible level. Bear in mind that the central idea in the Gospels is that a man should pass from a lower to a higher state and that this is inner evolution or re-birth. Since the "Word of God" is teaching about the means necessary for this inner evolution, all intellectual temptation in the Gospels refers to a man's private thoughts about the Truth of the *Word*, and the truth of the *senses*, and all emotional temptation is about self-love and the love of God. There is, naturally, disagreement between the lower and the higher level, just as we might say there is disagreement between a seed and a plant. We might say that a seed can live for itself and be full of its self-love or it can surrender itself and its self-will to the higher influences that seek to operate on it, so that it becomes, by transformation, a plant.

The third temptation is given in these words in Luke:

"And he led him to Jerusalem, and set him on the pinnacle of the temple, and said unto him, If thou art the Son of God, cast thyself down from hence: for it is written, He shall give his angels charge concerning thee, to guard thee: and, on their hands they shall bear thee up, lest haply thou dash thy foot against a stone. And Jesus answering said unto him, It is said, Thou shalt not tempt the Lord thy God."   (Luke iv, 9–12.)

It can be understood that the self-love necessarily only worships itself. So it can and actually does ascribe divineness to itself. That is, the lower imagines it is the higher and so tempts God. It cannot feel its own nothingness and so swells itself up to heaven; and then in the intoxication of its own divinity, in the madness of self-illusion, it may attempt the impossible and destroy itself.

In the accounts of the temptation by the devil it is said that Christ was led by the spirit into the wilderness. In Luke, he was "led by the spirit in the wilderness

THE IDEA OF TEMPTATION IN THE GOSPELS

during forty days being tempted of the devil." In Mark, the expression is stronger:
"And straightway the spirit driveth him forth into the wilderness, and he was in
the wilderness forty days tempted of Satan; and he was with the wild beasts."
(Mark i, 12–13.) In Matthew: "Then was Jesus led up of the spirit into the
wilderness to be tempted of the devil" (Matt. iv, 1). The temptations in the wilderness, in each Gospel where they are described, are made to follow on the baptism
of Jesus by John. It seems strange that Christ should be led into temptation by
the very spirit of inner illumination with which he was filled. But Christ taught
that a man must be born again of the spirit; and without temptation there is no
transformation. The spirit is the connecting medium between higher and lower.
The human in Christ had to be transformed and lifted up to the divine level.
And since the spirit is the intermediary, drawing the lower by a series of transformations to the higher, the work of the spirit is to lead a man into the wilderness
—nay, rather, into utter bewilderment—and subject him to being tempted by
every element in himself so that all that is useless for his self-evolution is put
behind him and all that can grow and understand is put in front. The devil
represents all in a man that cannot evolve and all that does not wish to and hates
every idea of inner evolution, all that wishes only to slander and misunderstand
and have its own way. All this must gradually be put behind a man who seeks
real inner development and not allowed to take the first place and control him.
That is, the order of things in a man must change and what is first become last.
So in one of the accounts Christ is made to say to the devil: "Get thee behind
me Satan." That this new inner order in a man which is brought about by
temptation cannot take place at once is clear from Luke's words, where it is said
that the temptations of Christ were not ended. "The devil", it is said, "departed
from him for a season."

Chapter Three

THE MARRIAGE AT CANA

BETWEEN whom was the Marriage? Notice nothing is said about the bride and groom. Jesus and his Mother surely are externally represented by Mother and Son: understood psychologically, it is about an internal union of natural and spiritual in Jesus. Why, then, does not the Master of the Feast realise what has taken place? Why was it impossible for him to understand, so much so that the servants did not attempt to inform him, although technically the servants were presumably under the orders of the Master of the Feast? Because a *new Master* has appeared—almost secretly—and notice that this new Master does not say anything to the Master of the Feast, whom we may term the *old Master*. When Man changes his whole psychology in such a profound way the former Master of it is no longer in control but another and greater Master appears. By self-mastery as regards the natural side of him represented by the Mother, Jesus reached a stage in which the old Master had no longer any power—and yet did not know what had happened. Jesus is not Master of the Feast—but no one tells the former Master what has taken place. They are all *silent*. There is no rivalry —only *silence*. A transformation has taken place actually in terms of water into wine. But nothing happened through violence. In all the miracles of Jesus, there was never violence or rivalry. There was, in place, *silence*. Jesus told Pilate that if necessary he, Jesus, could call powers into action that would bring about his release. But he did not use them. Violence breeds violence. And it is a strange line of thought that leads to reflection upon what is master in oneself and how to overcome, or rather, to turn aside from it. Nothing must be said to antagonise and inflame it. Even Pilate could see a little about Jesus: and the Master of the Feast could appreciate a good wine. But no doubt the latter would have been a difficult factor to handle if the miracle had been explained by his servants and the Master's authority disputed.

There are many things said in the Gospels about this inner *silence*, in con-nexion with changing oneself: silence in oneself is required: "Let not thy left

28

hand know what thy right hand doeth" (Matt. vi, 3). One does not overcome earthly authority by reacting violently to it. A man may react violently to his father. How many throw away their best side in violently opposing authority? They even become what they hate—in time. Inner change is not gained in this way. But here, in this symbolic marriage, the authority of the Mother of Jesus is not represented in terms of a reaction but as a bringing about of some inner ordering, whereby her significance is not destroyed but used aright—because it is she who makes it possible for the miracle to take place by telling the "servants" to obey what Jesus told them to do. And since he derived from her his human or natural side it seems clear that, at this stage of his development, he has brought the human or natural side in him into a right relation with the greater or spiritual side—and so "she" obeyed "him". There are disciplines where this "natural" side is taken as something to be overcome entirely and only spiritual thought, far above the earthly side, is allowed. This cutting-in-half of a man or woman cannot be regarded as an ordering or harmony of all the notes that sound in our Being. Jesus, on his Mother's side, was born a man. His task was to connect Man with God—the natural with the spiritual—and not to cut asunder into opposites what are not opposites at all, but different levels and scales.

Now the "natural" side of a man and the more internal side—or relatively spiritual side—might similarly be represented by two figures, or by two rooms, one opening into the other, or by two heights, lower and higher, or by two towns, or in many other ways. The visual imagery by itself is nothing. The significance is everything, for there lies the meaning. It is not the visual imagery in a parable that means what the parable means. It is not words used in a parable that mean what the parable means. Some dreams are pure parables, as are some ancient myths and stories. But it is the meaning that such parables, myths, dreams, fairy-stories, conduct, that is the significant thing. To the natural level of mind they appear without meaning, save a literal one. But the spiritual, the psychological, meaning, cannot be conveyed directly in words to the natural level. And this is why *another language* has always existed. A verbal language can only be understood by those familiar with it, but a parable in visual representation can be understood by people not speaking the same verbal language. There are *two* languages: they correspond to *two* depths or levels in Man.

Now there is a term used in esoteric language which always signifies that a certain development has been fulfilled. This term is numerical. The number *three* implies *fulfilment*. In this *sign* of *Water into Wine*, it is said at the beginning that *on the third day* there was a marriage. The beginning, middle and end form the completion of a stage. So in esoteric language the number three is the end of something and the beginning of something else. When a psychological stage has been fulfilled, a new stage begins. This is the "third day". The old is passing away, the new state beginning. Or, the higher level is beginning to be active and the former level is beginning to obey this new higher level. The number *three* is used to represent this situation as, for example, when Christ fulfilled his necessary time in hell and rose on the *third* day. There are many examples of this use of the number *three* in the esoteric books of the Bible. Jonah was three days in the belly of the great fish. Peter denies Christ three times—that is, fully. Christ asks Peter three times if he loves him. The fig-tree that did not bear fruit for three years was to be cut down. There are many other examples of the use of the number three as meaning fulfilment, either fulfilment in the sense of a new beginning or fulfilment as the completion of a thing.

Now the whole *sign* of *Water into Wine* is about a stage that Jesus had reached in the development of his human side. So it begins with "the third day":

"And upon the third day there was a marriage in Cana of Galilee, and the mother of Jesus was there: and Jesus also was bidden, and his disciples, to the marriage. And when the wine failed, the mother of Jesus saith unto him, They have no wine. And Jesus saith unto her, Woman, what have I to do with thee? Mine hour is not yet come. His mother saith unto the servants, Whatsoever he saith unto you, do it. Now there were six waterpots of stone set there after the Jews' manner of purifying, containing two or three firkins apiece. Jesus saith unto them, Fill the waterpots with water. And they filled them up to the brim. And he saith unto them, Draw out now, and bear unto the ruler of the feast. And they bare it. And when the ruler of the feast tasted the water now become wine, and knew not whence it was (but the servants which had drawn the water knew), the ruler of the feast calleth on the bridegroom and saith unto him, Every man setteth on first the good wine; and when men have drunk freely, then that which is worse: thou hast kept the good wine until now. This beginning of his signs did Jesus in Cana of Galilee, and manifested his glory; and his disciples believed on him." (John ii, 1–11.)

Notice that the Mother of Jesus is present, representing his former level, with which he is still in contact, but he has nothing to do with it. To the former level of himself he says: "Woman, what have I to do with thee?" To understand his rough attitude towards his Mother, it is necessary to look at some other passages in the Gospels. Let us suppose a man reaches a level at which self-pity —all that is pathetic in him—has been destroyed. Many people regard Christ as a pathetic figure—a *sick* Christ. This conception of Christ usually goes with the view that he was brutally treated and dragged to the Cross. Of course, everything in the Gospels shows quite the opposite. The Gospels show that he deliberately suffered on the Cross. He predicted his crucifixion. He told his disciples that he had to undergo this fulfilment of his end. And although he prayed in the agony at Gethsemane that this end might be altered, calling it a cup that he must drink, he said: "Nevertheless not as I will but as thou wilt." To take him as a pathetic figure is beside the point. The sentimental Christ is an invention. It is obvious that he was harsh in his handling of others, many of whom he offended, and he was harsh with himself. In the scene with Pilate it is shown that if he followed his own will he could escape. He says to Pilate. "Thou couldest have no power over me except it were given thee from above" (John xix, 11). But he deliberately plays the role allotted to him and carries it out because this was the aim that was set him to fulfil, as he so often explained. The disciples did not understand and only later some of them grasped the *idea* of the whole drama of Christ enacted visibly before them—namely, the inevitable crucifixion of a higher level of Truth at the hands of those on a lower level. The destruction of psychological Truth by literal truth is the continual drama of human life.

* * *

Jesus says to his Mother: "Woman, what have I to do with thee? Mine hour is not yet come?" This suggests that eventually he will be destroyed by what the "Mother" represents in humanity. We must get entirely away from any literal sense, even from any actual figure. Jesus had reached a point in his own evolution and temptation where the "Mother" level scarcely has anything to do with him—that is, some level typified by the "Mother"—whom he calls *Woman*. It no longer has power and yet still has power but is subordinate. So Jesus changes water into wine and so gives the first *sign* of the level of inner development that he has reached. The two ideas are connected—the raising of himself from the "Mother" level and the resulting power of turning "water" into "wine". But it is clear from the account of the marriage feast—which is a psychological portrait—that although Jesus had reached this new state, in which he had nothing more to do with his former state, yet the former state is close beneath him and still can take power. He controls it so that the "Mother" understands that obedience is necessary. So she orders the "servants" to obey what Jesus commands. Three levels in Jesus are thus depicted. The lowest is represented by the "servants" —who obey the "Mother", the middle by the "Mother", the highest by the new level or state of Jesus where the "Mother" obeys. Let us conceive these three states as three horizontal lines drawn one above the other in parallel. The middle line will then represent the intermediary between the highest and lowest lines. In other words, some definite order of levels is indicated—highest, middle and lowest. This state, attained by Jesus and marking the beginning of his power of teaching, is defined by the general setting of the psychological portrait in terms of a *marriage*—that is, some inner union, totally different from the Mother–Son union—and its consequences, the turning of water into wine.

What is meant in this psychological description by the idea of a marriage? What element in Jesus had come into union with some other element, with the result that water became wine and so gave the first *sign* of his inner evolution? In the Bible, the first Truths concerning our existence and what we have to do— that is, the Commandments—were written on tables of stone, as we are told. But we must recall that something apparently went wrong in the transmission of these Truths from God to Moses. Moses cast down the original tables ("written by God") and smashed them, when he found that in his absence on Mount Sinai his people had begun to worship a golden calf that they had set up:

"And Moses turned, and went down from the mount, with the two tables of the testimony in his hand; tables that were written on both their sides; on the one side and on the other were they written. And the tables were the work of God, and the writing was the writing of God, graven upon the tables. . . . And it came to pass, as soon as he came nigh unto the camp, that he saw the calf and the dancing: and Moses' anger waxed hot, and he cast the tables out of his hands, and brake them beneath the mount."

(Exodus xxxii, 15, 16, 19.)

Then Moses was commanded by God to make two more tables of stone with his own hands. "And he hewed two tables of stone like unto the first." (Exodus xxxiv, 4.) All Truth coming from those who are at a far higher level of the understanding of it than we are cannot be transmitted directly. We have nothing with which to receive it—and so occupy ourselves with our level of understanding Truth, with legal agreements, forms, and so on. Higher Truth therefore reaches us in terms of lower, rigid, literal Truth. It is adults speaking to children. It is impossible to convey the full meaning.

Just as the Ten Commandments had to be represented on stone tables so that the Children of Israel could receive them, so the already existing Truth, the water, in this parable, is described as poured into six water-pots of stone, those used "for the Jewish rites of purification". This suggests that the Truth was based on the ancient Jewish beliefs and customs. *Six* is in ancient allegory the number of Creation, or, on different levels, the number of preparation for any achievement. For six days in the week we prepare for the Sabbath; a Jewish servant had to serve for six years before he won his freedom; a vineyard had to be pruned for six years; the land had to be sown for six years, but the seventh year was always a "sabbath of solemn rest for the land"—such was the law given to Moses. Likewise there were six steps up to the throne of Solomon. Thus the six water-pots of stone would appear to stand for a period of preparation during which the Truth as water had been received and held in the minds of the Jews and had taken a form corresponding to their ancient faith, awaiting its transformation at the Coming of Christ.

Now, in this parable, "water", after having been poured into "stone" jars, becomes "wine". Let us recall what has been said already about these three stages of Truth—stone, water, wine. Stone represents literal Truth, and we can conceivably understand that successive transformations of meaning are implied in these different levels of Truth. What we are taught at our mother's knee may be Truth, but it is not our own even though we obey it. God is a spirit: the "Mother" is not. The authority is not yet internal but has come from outside.

33

It is said elsewhere that Jesus taught as one *having authority*. But even this seeing the truth of Truth is not sufficient and not only meant here. A further stage is meant—and we must seek for the word Good in order to gain an idea of the meaning. Stone, water, wine, indicate three levels of Truth, but where can we find any word comparable to Good? We find it at the end of this dynamic portrait. The Ruler of the Feast, tasting the water made into wine, remarks that the usual custom of the world at a marriage feast is to give the good wine first and the poorer afterwards. He was speaking literally:

> "And when the ruler of the feast tasted the water now become wine, and knew not whence it was (but the servants which had drawn the water knew), the ruler of the feast calleth the bridegroom, and saith unto him, Every man setteth on first the good wine; and when men have drunk freely, then that which is worse: thou hast kept the good wine until now."

Now the "Mother" had told the servants to obey "Christ". Let us notice that the servants knew and the "Mother" knew they had been ordered to pour *water* into the empty stone jars. They had access to the *water*—that is, the part of Jesus that was at that level of understanding. He *used* that lower level—not directly. He used it through the intermediary middle level, called "Mother". Here we have real psychology—something long ago lost. But the whole mind must be abstracted from the senses—the level of literal meaning—to catch a single flash from the brilliance of inner psychological meaning in this first sign of the inner development of Jesus recorded in terms of a visible imagery, palpably false. Consider, only, if these visible images meant what they stand for literally, then why did Jesus transform about 120 gallons of water into wine, as we are told? In a small village, such as Cana of Galilee was, this would be absurd. It cannot mean that so much water was miraculously made into wine, equal to some six hundred litres, towards the end of a local festival. But it is exactly through seeing that the meaning cannot be literal, that we can begin to look for another meaning that is psychological. The representation of the psychological in terms of physical images, as in cartoons, is one thing: but the taking of psychological meaning in terms of the physical is a reverse process that continually occurs in every attempt to convey higher meaning. So Christ—as psychological meaning— is always crucified by those who only can take in literal, sense-based meaning.

A sense-based mind believes that the Bread and Wine used in the ritual of the commemoration of the Last Supper are to be taken literally. But the literal level of comprehension in such high matters plays havoc with us and has done so throughout the ages. A man may take the phrase: "Thou shalt not kill", literally and obey it as such. But if he sees more deeply and understands that he may be killing others *psychologically* all day, in his thoughts and feelings, he will begin to pass to another level of the understanding of this injunction and realise the fuller or more internal meaning of it. Then what he has been taught outwardly begins to penetrate him and its meaning undergoes an inner transformation comparable at first to stone into water, and eventually, when he realises the Good contained in the command and so has compassion, which is of Goodness, to water into wine. Through this insight, he will *evolve* in himself—in his understanding. Individual evolution is only possible by transformation of the understanding, a man being his understanding and what he wills from it and nothing more. A man is not physical. Only psychologically can anyone individually evolve in the sense of the Gospels. Once a man has seen for himself the value of what he has been taught as mere command or outer Truth, once the emotional side of him has developed up to whatever knowledge of Truth he has, so that he seeks to *do* what he *knows* from his own willing and feeling and consent, he is then another kind of man, an evolving man, a man reaching the stage that we are taking at present as wine, a New Man.

★   ★   ★

One of the deepest teachings of esotericism deals with the union of the two sides of a man. In the esoteric teaching of the Greeks exemplified by Socrates this idea runs through the whole exposition of Man as an unfinished creation of a possible higher state of himself. Plato calls these two sides Knowledge and Being. He says: "The true lover of knowledge is always striving after being" (*Republic*). And again he says: "When it (the soul) is stayed upon that on which truth and being are shining, it understands and knows and is seen to have reason. . . . This, then, which imparts truth to the things that are known and the power of knowing to the knower, is what I would have you term the idea of good. . . . The good may be said to be not only the author of knowledge of all things known but of their being and essence" (*Republic*, 508, 509). A man must have being in order to know rightly. The education of being and the education of knowledge was Plato's greatest theme in his later books. How to bring up people rightly and how to give them knowledge and at what time to give them knowledge—this was the problem with which he was continually occupied. To give poor types of people knowledge that they will only misuse was one thing that Plato saw clearly as a great danger. To open knowledge of whatever kind to everyone was to him a crime. He saw clearly that many disciplines must be undergone referring to character and being before a man was fit to be taught knowledge. In fact, he came to the conclusion that for anyone to be taught great knowledge he must have been trained in all the exercises and disciplines of life until he had become of an age that was no longer that of youth. In the esoteric schools of which we can see traces in ancient literature, many very severe disciplines existed before a candidate was allowed to receive esoteric knowledge. He might have to serve in a most menial position for years, subject to insults that were a test on the side of being. If he passed these tests successfully and developed in himself strength and patience he was allowed to receive some knowledge. But if he broke, if he pitied himself, if he complained, if he was weak in his being, if he lied, if he behaved maliciously, if he took advantage of others, if he was resentful, if he thought he was better than other people, he received no knowledge. This means that the side of his being was tested first before he was given knowledge. To-day the situation is quite different. Anyone is given knowledge without discrimination and there is a growing class of literature calling attention to this point, without the idea of the development of being as a primary factor being quite understood.

* * *

For a man to receive Higher Knowledge he must have good Being to make salt in him. If we regard knowledge as chlorine and being as sodium, then unless a man has enough sodium in him to combine with the chlorine he receives from outside he will not have salt in him. Then the chlorine poisons him. The poisonous power of knowledge alone without the good ground, of which the Gospels so often speak, to receive it, may simply produce world-poison. In such a case the acquiring of knowledge can only produce the worst results. But the mystery is deeper than this. The esoteric teaching about knowledge and being refers to the fact that knowledge cannot be understood unless there is a corresponding development of being. A man may know a great deal and understand nothing because his being is not equal to his knowledge. As a consequence, no inner union can take place between his being and his knowledge. We see to-day an extraordinary number of books full of knowledge but with no understanding. We see the cheapest explanations given of the facts of science. The man of poor being and great knowledge can only give out meaningless material that leads nowhere. And not only this, but he can only complicate everything and make it unintelligible. And so science to-day complicates everything too much and apparently leads nowhere. Countless scientists are writing papers that no one understands, not even the scientists. The reason for this is that the conditions of knowledge are no longer understood because the side of being is ignored. Esotericism has always understood the conditions of knowledge. It has always understood that knowledge should always lead to understanding and that under-standing is only possible with a corresponding development of being. This is the deepest idea concerning human psychology for then a union takes place that leads to inner evolution. In this marriage or union, the meaning of the knowledge unites with the being of the person and leads to his inner development. This is what the Parable of Water made into Wine is about. It means that Christ united his knowledge with the Good of his being. His knowledge and the goodness of his being became one. Let us repeat what has already been pointed out, that the Ruler of the Feast speaks about the *good* wine and that the Good came last. First of all, a man must be taught Truth or knowledge and then the Goodness of it comes later. Actually, however, Good must also precede knowledge, but of this we will speak later. What is good is prior to all Truth but in time it seems as if knowledge comes first. The ultimate aim in life is the Good. If we say that at the summit of things is Good then it is prior to everything else and so is first in scale, but in time it looks as if knowledge comes first. All knowledge should lead to Good. Therefore Good is first in scale, although to our senses, which are in time and only see a cross section of all existence called the present moment, it looks the other way round.

For a parallel idea see Appendix.

Chapter Four

THE IDEA OF GOOD BEING ABOVE TRUTH

PART ONE

O N several occasions it is recorded in the Gospels that Christ offended the Pharisees by breaking the Sabbath day. This made them especially furious. It seemed to them that even to do good on the Sabbath day was prohibited by their religious laws and scruples. The term *Pharisee* refers to the inner state of a man who acts only from external laws and prohibitions for the sake of appearances and feels merit in keeping them, in contrast with that of a man who acts genuinely from what is good. This difference is brought out in many illustrations in the Gospels, as in the case of the Good Samaritan who had compassion on the wounded man who had been attacked by robbers whereas the priest and Levite had passed by on the other side. But the difference is particularly emphasised where the attitude of the Pharisees towards the Sabbath is used as a background. On one occasion in the synagogue Christ healed a man with a withered right hand on the Sabbath. The right hand is mentioned because it represents, in the ancient language of parables, power to do—and so power to do good. The image is used to represent the Pharisees themselves; their power of doing good was withered. Before Christ healed the man, he looked round and said to all those present: "I ask you, is it lawful on the sabbath to do good?" The attitude of the Pharisees was that the religious laws must be kept literally. Notice that Christ here is not speaking of Truth but of Good. Which is to come first? The quotation from Luke is as follows:

"And it came to pass on another sabbath, that he entered into the synagogue and taught: and there was a man there, and his right hand was withered. And the scribes and Pharisees watched him, whether he would heal on the sabbath; that they might find out how to accuse him. But he knew their thoughts; and he said to the man that had his hand withered, Rise up, and stand forth in the midst. And he arose and stood forth. And Jesus said unto them, I ask you, Is it lawful on the sabbath to do good, or to do harm? to save a life, or to destroy it? And he looked round about on them all, and said unto him, Stretch forth thy hand. And he did so: and his hand was restored. But they were filled with madness; and communed one with another what they might do to Jesus."

(Luke vi, 6–11.)

It is clear that this incident has to do with acting primarily from *what is Good*, apart from any other considerations. Christ is putting what is Good above what is Truth. To the Pharisees Truth was the Mosaic Law and the commandments, which, taken literally, forbid work on the sabbath: ". . . six days shalt thou labour and do all thy work: but the seventh day is a sabbath unto the Lord thy God: in it thou shalt do no manner of work. . . ." The Pharisees put Truth above Good. What have we to understand here? What great issues lie behind this narrative? We know from history that all religious quarrels and persecutions have arisen from matters of doctrine—that is, from the side of *what is the Truth*—the side of knowledge and opinion, alone. If all mankind were charitable, if everyone acted from Good, no such quarrels and persecutions would have arisen. If everyone loved his neighbour as much as himself, through the light of his love of God as the source of supreme Good, no one would kill or steal or bear false witness and so on. In fact, the decalogue of Moses—the ten commandments written on tables of stone—would not have any significance. But to the Pharisees, who lived by the law and did not *understand* anything, what was written down was more to them than any meaning behind the letter. If Man were entirely good, no laws or commandments would be necessary; he would not need to learn any truths, any knowledge. He could not commit murder, because he would know from Good that it was impossible to do so. How can you do good to your neighbour by murdering him? How can you do good to him by stealing from him? The last five commandments are knowledge about Good. The end of all knowledge is only one thing: what is Good? There is no other end or meaning in knowledge but Good. But to-day this is lost sight of and people believe that knowledge by itself leads to its own end. This is a mistake. All knowledge should lead to Good. To what end is mere knowledge leading mankind to-day? Now if it is asked why is Truth necessary at all, the answer is, that Man is not *good*—that is, his

39

level of Good is very low. And there is only one way to raise the level of Good in a man. A man's level of Good can only be raised by *knowledge of Truth about a better Good*. To raise himself he must learn Truth. What kind of Truth? He must be taught and learn and practise knowledge of Truth that belongs to a higher Good than the level of Good that represents him. For each person represents in himself a certain level of Good. To gain a new level of Good, he must first proceed by knowledge. Through learning or knowledge—that is, through knowledge of the Truth about how to reach a higher level of Good—if he sincerely tries to act from it and see its truth and meaning for himself—he reaches a new level of Good, that is, a new level of himself. Once he has reached this level, at which the Good of all he has learned as knowledge becomes active, he need no longer bother about the steps in knowledge that led him to the stage he has attained. As a rough and inadequate metaphor, a man while climbing a mountain must use his knowledge of climbing. Once he has reached the summit, he sees everything in a new way. He sees the new relationship of everything from the height he has reached and need not think what means he had to use to get to that point. The Mosaic Law, or, at least, the ten commandments, are instructions from the side of Truth, as to how to attain a level of Good, where, as commandments, they have no further meaning. But if they are taken as an *end*, and not as a means to an end, they become stumbling blocks.

Christ, then, in the passage quoted above, is speaking from Good and not from literal Truth: and the Pharisees condemn him and hate him because they hold only to the literal Truth. Truth about a higher level can be taken as Truth *at the level of Good a man is at*—at his own level. A man then sees this Truth, that is designed to lead to a higher level of Good, in terms of the level of Good he is at. If his level of Good is self-interest and self-love, he can twist the higher Truth to suit his vanity, as do all Pharisees in every age. That is, he can entirely misconceive its meaning. What is called the Word of God in the Gospels is Truth about what is necessary for the reaching of a higher level of Good—that is, what is necessary for *inner evolution*, for all inner evolution is reaching higher Good through knowledge. The problem of the relation of Truth and Good thus becomes clearer. A new level of Good in Man cannot be reached directly. It can only be reached by instruction about how to reach it and instruction must take the form of Truth about this higher level of Good. That is, it must come, first of all, in the form of *knowledge* which a man must learn and apply to his life. Knowledge about higher Good must come *first* as teaching. When it has fulfilled its object, when a man through knowledge of the Truth as to how to reach a higher level of Good has reached this new Good by trying to live it sincerely by his own inner efforts, then this Truth or knowledge, which came *first*, is replaced by the resulting Good itself; and thereafter the Truth or knowledge that led him to this new state takes the *second* place, having fulfilled its object as a conductor to a higher level. That is, what was *first* becomes *second* in order and what was *second* in order now *becomes first*. A *reversal* takes place. Truth first takes the place of Good: and then Good takes the place of Truth. Actually the six days of labour in the *genesis of a man* and the seventh day of rest represent six stages of knowledge followed by the reaching of Good itself, which is called the Sabbath. So many things, both in the Old and the New Testaments, are said about this *reversal of order* or about the first being last and the last first that it is remarkable that they have not been more generally understood, in so far as the *psychology* underlying real teaching about Man and his inner evolution is concerned. People, however, cling to Truth as an end and so feel their doctrinal differences, whether religious or political, most easily. In the Old Testament, there is the strange story of Jacob imitating or taking the place of Esau, to mention one example of Truth first taking the place of Good. Jacob impersonated Esau by putting goatskins on his hands and neck, for his brother was represented as being covered with hair. He went to his father Isaac, who was almost blind, with an offering of venison, and said: "I am Esau thy first-born; I have done according as thou badest me: arise, I pray thee, sit and eat of my venison, that thy soul may bless me." And Isaac gave him the blessing that belonged to his elder son, Esau. Good is really first, for God himself is defined and only defined as Good. So it is first-born. But to reach Good, truth must come first, so Jacob takes the place of Esau. Then again, take the curious story of Perez and Zerah, the twin sons of Judah, whose birth is described thus:

"And it came to pass . . . that one put out a hand: and the midwife took and bound upon his hand a scarlet thread, saying, This came out first. And it came to pass, as he drew back his hand, that, behold, his brother came out: and she said, Wherefore hast thou made a breach for thyself? therefore his name was called Perez. And afterward came out his brother, that had the scarlet thread upon his hand: and his name was called Zerah." (Genesis xxxviii, 28–30.)

Why should this be recorded, unless it has some deeper meaning? Again, there is the strange story of Manasseh, the first-born, and Ephraim, the second-born, the twin children of Joseph, who were brought to Jacob to be blessed:

"And Joseph took them both, Ephraim in his right hand toward Israel's left hand, and Manasseh in his left hand towards Israel's right hand . . . And Israel stretched out his right hand, and laid it upon Ephraim's head, who was the younger, and his left hand upon Manasseh's head, guiding his hands wittingly; for Manasseh was the first-born." (Thus Jacob put his hands cross-wise.) "And Joseph said unto his father, Not so, my father: for this is the first-born; put thy right hand upon his head. And his father refused . . ."
(Genesis xlviii, 13, 14, 18, 19.)

Here then is a *crossing* or *reversal* of hands. If you realise that Truth must come first in any inner development and Good comes as a result, and that then Good comes first and Truth becomes second, you will grasp one meaning of this *crossing of hands*. All these allegories refer to the *psychological situation* of Man now on earth in relation to his possible evolution. Man on earth now can no longer be taught Good directly. But he is still capable of being taught Good through *knowledge of Truth*.

PART TWO

DID mankind ever act from Good? The ancient allegory in Genesis where it is said that "The whole earth was of one language and one speech," has already been quoted. This refers to an age when men acted from Good—for Good only can give a common language or agreement. There was a time when men did not act from theories of right and wrong, from different ideas of Truth, from different doctrines, from different aspects of knowledge. They acted, first, from the inner recognition of what is good. This united everyone; for Good is the only power that can *unite*. All harmony is from Good. As long as Good came first, everything else did not matter. A man might hold this view or that, as best suited him, but by putting God first he was in agreement with everyone else who put Good first. The description that Mankind once spoke with *one* tongue means that there was a stage of Man where Good was in the first place, and so everyone spoke a common language. A stage of degeneration followed, represented by the building of the Tower of Babel to reach to Heaven:

"And the whole earth was of one language and of one speech. And it came to pass, as they journeyed from the east, that they found a plain in the land of Shinar; and they dwelt there. And they said one to another, Go to, let us make brick, and burn them throughly. And they had brick for stone, and slime they had for mortar, And they said, Go to, let us build us a city, and a tower, whose top may reach unto heaven."   (Genesis xi, 1-4.)

Then follows an allegorical description of how they began to misunderstand one another, represented by their speaking in different languages, and how they were scattered.

The first verse: "And the whole earth was of one language and one speech" means that once Mankind were in a certain state of unity on earth. The second verse: "And it came to pass, as they journeyed from the east, that they found a plain in the land of Shinar; and they dwelt there" means that they began to move away from that state of unity—i.e. they "journeyed from the east". They moved away from the source of the state of unity and so at the same time descended in their level of being—i.e. "they found a plain and dwelt there". They then began to invent notions of their own, being no longer in contact with the original source—i.e. "Come, let us make bricks . . . and they had bricks for stone and slime for mortar". Stone, as we have seen, represents Truth. They had no longer Truth: "they had bricks for stone"—that is, something made by Man in place of the Word of God. Here they had bricks for stone. Having lost the stone—i.e. the truths originally taught—they propose to burn bricks for themselves and build for themselves. They had slime for mortar—i.e. something evil in place of something good. They propose to raise a tower even to heaven—that is, to raise themselves to the level of God. Everything based on the self-love wishes to raise itself up, for the self-love only seeks to possess and have power over everything. It wishes to exalt itself—hence the image of the *tower* in the above parable. All this and what follows means that Man began to think that *he himself* was the source of Good, and not God. He committed the spiritual act called *theft*, which is referred to in the eighth commandment: "Thou shalt not steal". He attributed to *himself* that which did not belong to him and of which he was not the cause. And this psychological *theft* has continued, until to-day it has reached a remarkable growth, so much so that people tacitly attribute everything, even life, to themselves. As a result of this original theft, Mankind no longer spoke a common language. The "confusion of tongues" took place. There was no longer a common language—that is, a man ceased to understand his neighbours, for there was no longer any common ground of understanding which only a common perception of Good can give. Babel replaced unity. This is the present state of things in the world, where Man attributes everything to himself and has no sense of any other idea of the Universe or of the meaning of Mankind on earth. He attributes mind, thought, consciousness, feeling, volition, life, and, in fact, everything, *to himself*, although he is and must always remain incapable of explaining any one of these things. And his only explanation of the Universe to-day is that it arose by chance, and that it is meaningless.

§II. THE MIRACLE AT THE POOL OF BETHESDA

This miracle is given only in the Gospel of John. The language of this Gospel is emotional. It is a very strange Gospel. It is quite wrong to suppose that we can understand it merely by reading it through once or twice. No one really knows for certain who the author is or when it was written. The portrait of Jesus Christ given in this Gospel is different from that given in the first three Gospels, or so-called synoptic Gospels. The latter are called synoptic, not because they were written down by eye-witnesses—for Luke and Mark never saw Christ—but because, in a vague way, their historical narratives see "eye-to-eye". But when we come to the Gospel of John it is obvious that there is no attempt made to render the record of Christ's ministry on earth into a progressive historical narrative. Who was this John, whose name is appended to this Gospel? When was it published? No one can, for certain, answer these questions. Was the writer of this Gospel really the John mentioned who leaned on the bosom of Jesus, the disciple whom Jesus loved? Again it is impossible to say. The whole language of this Gospel is strange and in a certain sense the figure of Jesus Christ appears in a strange light. Also the very few miracles related in it, beginning with the Transformation of Water into Wine (given in no other Gospel), are all strange. They are related in curiously full detail. Among other things, they are characterised by the use of number-language or numerology.

Let us begin by taking the long account of the miracle performed by Jesus at the Pool of Bethesda. This miracle, given only here, is the third miracle related in John, having been preceded by the Transformation of Water into Wine and the Healing of the Nobleman's Son at Capernaum.

"After all these things there was a feast of the Jews; and Jesus went up to Jerusalem. Now there is in Jerusalem by the sheep-gate a pool, which is called in Hebrew Bethesda, having five porches. In these lay a multitude of them that were sick, blind, halt, withered, And a certain man was there, which had been thirty and eight years in his infirmity. When Jesus saw him lying, and knew that he had been now a long time in that case, he said unto him, Wouldest thou be made whole? The sick man answered him, Sir, I have no man, when the water is troubled, to put me into the pool: but while I am coming, another steppeth down before me. Jesus saith unto him, Arise, take up thy bed, and walk. And straightway the man was made whole, and took up his bed and walked. Now it was the Sabbath on that day. So the Jews said unto him that was cured, It is the Sabbath, and it is not lawful for thee to take up thy bed. But he answered them, He that made me whole, the same said unto me, Take up thy bed and walk. They asked him, Who is the Man who said unto thee, Take up thy bed, and walk? But he that was healed wist not who it was: for Jesus had conveyed himself away, a multitude being in the place. Afterward Jesus findeth him in the temple, and said unto him, Behold, thou art made whole: sin no more, lest a worse thing befall thee. The man went away, and told the Jews that it was Jesus which had made him whole. And for this cause did the Jews persecute Jesus, because he did these things on the Sabbath." (John v, 1–18.)

You will see that the whole of this miracle is divided into two parts. The first is about the actual miracle and the second part about the reaction of the Jews to the miracle. But the first part is again divided into two parts. Jesus says: "Wouldest thou be made whole?" And then he says: "Take up thy bed and walk". Now let us look at the various things said before the miracle takes place, for we may be quite sure, in regard to the ancient language of parables, that everything said has a particular significance. A multitude lie sick in a certain place, called a "gate for sheep", and this has five porches. In these five porches lie a multitude of "them that were sick, blind, halt, and withered". We know already that in the language of parables the sick, the halt, the paralysed and so on, represent psychological states. Now in the miracles given in John's Gospel, the number *five* occurs again in connexion with the Woman of Samaria, who had five husbands, and to whom Christ spoke at the Well. He told her she had had five husbands and that her present husband was not her real husband: and then he spoke to her of "living water"— that is, living Truth—which, Christ said, if once a man drank of it he should not thirst. And she said: "Sir, give me this water, that I thirst not, neither come all the way hither to draw" (John iv, 15). When we receive teaching that is not of the external world at all—that is, not of the five senses, which render to us the external world, the world of the senses—it is a matter of the greatest difficulty to accept it. And even if we do accept it, we still live very close to the five senses—that is, we still remain close to all the ideas belonging to the external world as rendered by our senses which we cannot help taking for *reality*. The senses give us time and space, for example, and we think in terms of time and space and cannot get beyond this sense-based thinking. Our deepest thought is beyond all time and space. But our ordinary thought is, as it were, framed in terms of time and in terms of space and we do not know how to think *in a new way*, apart from these sensible categories. Even if we assent to the idea of eternity, where there is no time or space, we cannot grasp it. Even if we hear of a teaching that lies beyond the categories of time and space, we cannot grasp its eternal meaning because we cannot think in terms of timelessness or spacelessness. So we lie close to the five porches of the senses and although knowing another kind of teaching and even seeing its Truth yet we cannot get away from the power of the external world and its sense-given reality. Here, then, lie the multitude of those who have entered into the sheep gate, and remain close to the porches of the five senses. And they are crippled, being neither in one world nor another. So they are sick, blind, lame and withered, for they cannot psychologically move one way or the other. Yet their eyes are fastened on the miraculous waters of the pool, which at intervals is stirred into life, and they are healed one by one, according to their power of getting into the pool when the angel stirs it. The pool—that is, the waters—means as always in the language of parables the Truth of the Word. All these people gathered round the Truth of the Word of God cannot get into it properly. They are too close to the realities of life, to the visible appearance of things—that is, *to thought based on sense*. We are like the multitude of those lying close to the five porches in the miracle, awaiting something to strike belief into living meaning. And here lie all who have accepted Truth of a higher order which demands a new way of thinking, and who still are close to their ordinary way of thinking; they have accepted the *Word*, the Truth about inner evolution and re-birth, and cannot *do* it. So they lie, close to natural truth and yet looking at spiritual Truth and as it were in between two orders of Truth, the truth of the five senses and the Truth of the Word of God. So the man in the miracle is represented as lying in a bed. Psychologically a man lies in his beliefs and opinions. He lies in the Truth he has received but cannot walk in it—that is, he cannot live and do it. So Christ says: "Take up thy bed and *walk*." Christ represents here the power that can be given to a man to walk in, to live, to do, what he knows is the Truth. Jesus takes the place of the angel stirring the water of Truth and making it living Truth. Jesus always represents, in miracles, the power of Good acting on Truth and making it living. A man can only make Truth alive by seeing its Good, and if he perceives the Good of the Truth taught him, he acts spontaneously from his will. A man is internally both his Truth and his will. A man as Truth only acts slowly from Truth. But if he sees the Good of his Truth, he acts instantly from his will because his will passes instantly into what he perceives as Good, and only reluctantly into what he sees merely as Truth. The *whole* man is his Truth and his will passing into his Good. This is why the man in the Miracle of the Pool of Bethesda says to Jesus, when asked if he would be made whole: "Sir, I have no man, when the water is troubled, to put me into the pool: but while I am coming, another steppeth down before me." He describes his disease, which makes him psychologically halt, lame and withered. He is always *too slow*: he is always *second*, never first. A man who acts only from Truth is acting from what is second in him. If he acts from his will, he is acting from what is first in him. Jesus gives him the power of acting from his will—that is, power to take up the bed of Truth he lies in and walk and do it and live it. Jesus separates him from the world, from the power of the senses, and makes him see the Truth he has been taught in a living way. So the man is cured of his psychological disease— the disease of higher Truth being paralysed by lower Truth. All this was done on the *Sabbath*—that is, on a day which in the language of parables means complete separation from the world and its cares.

PART THREE

THE words *Christ* and *Jesus* have different meanings in the Gospels. We can be quite certain that every word used in the Gospels has its special significance which relates to the ancient language of parables. *Jesus* has one meaning: *Christ* has another meaning. The phrase *Jesus Christ* is used only twice in the Gospels, in each case by John. At all other times the name *Jesus* is used or the word *Christ*. Now *Christ* refers to the side of the Truth of the Word of God—that is, the Truth that can guide a man to inner self-evolution. And the word *Jesus* always refers to the Good of the truth. The Good and the Truth are united in *Jesus Christ*. In the words of John: "Grace and truth came by *Jesus Christ*" (John i, 17). The Gospel of John is written from Good or the marriage of Good with Truth. For this reason at the very beginning of John's Gospel the "grace and truth of Jesus Christ" are contrasted with the Truth (the "law of Moses") represented by John the Baptist, and almost immediately afterwards the marriage feast at Cana of Galilee follows with the Miracle of the Transformation of Water into Wine.

In this parable of the man miraculously healed at the Pool of Bethesda, it is said that *Jesus* spoke to him. That is, internally, the Good of the knowledge that the man had in him speaks to him. All teaching belonging to the higher level of Man must begin on the side of Truth before the Good of it can be realised. Here Jesus acts as the Good of the teaching about self-evolution, which the man knew of, because he was not quite in external life, but drawn back from its power, and so within the five porches and looking eagerly at the miraculous waters that can heal him. Jesus gives the man *the will to do* what he already knows as Truth by making him see the Good of it. And as all Truth must lead to its own Good, to be Truth, and as this takes place in stages, step by step, until the understanding of Truth leads to the final Good of it, so it is said that *Jesus*, representing the final realisation of the Good of the Truth, heals on the final or seventh day. So Jesus, as representing the Good of the teaching of Christ, heals on the Sabbath. The Jews are brought in here, as objecting, for many reasons, one being that they signify people who hold only to Truth itself and do not care about the Good to which it can lead. It does not mean here merely the Jews, as people who hold to the literal Mosaic Laws. It means far more than that. It means those who cannot get beyond knowledge as such and who dispute and argue from Truth, from doctrines and theories, and care nothing for Good itself. The Good of knowledge, the Good of Truth, is a stage very difficult to reach by anyone. But once a man reaches it, he begins to act from the final stage of Truth and the first stage of Good, when the meaning and inner sense and connexions of all he has been taught step by step passes into realisation, and Truth becomes transformed into the *Good of it*. The man no longer thinks now of the stages of Truth that have led him up to this higher level of Good—this clear inner perception of what is the Good of all he has learned. Now he will act instantly through the feeling of Good. He will not have to consult and remember the Truth. If Truth, if knowledge, does not lead to the *goodness* or *use* of it, which is its genuine partner, for what reason should we seek to study any Truth or knowledge? Knowledge is endless unless it leads to its own goal, which is its goodness. Good is the culmination of Truth. So Jesus as Good stands at the culmination of Truth, where it passes into the perception of its Good and find its true union. Here, as such, he performs always the miracles that transform Truth into Good—and so he cures the halt, lame, withered, blind—that is all those who stand only in Truth and cannot even begin to see that all doctrine, all Truth, all knowledge, must lead to Good to have any meaning. To follow knowledge alone, for its own sake, is to misunderstand not only the meaning of life and of oneself, but of the Universe. For the Universe, understood psychologically, is both the Truth of things and the Good of things. When a man acts from the sense of the Good of whatever Truth he knows, he acts directly from his will—from what he wants—for we *will* Good but *think* Truth.

In the Miracle at the Pool of Bethesda the man, feeling only the Truth of a teaching beyond the life of this world, could not bring his will or sense of Good to act *first*. He lay down close to the senses, close to the literal meaning of the Word of God. Yet he looked towards the miraculous meaning—the pool stirred by the angel—but could not grasp it. He *lay in Truth*—but could not *walk* upright in it. Jesus, as the Good of the Truth the man lay in, raises him up. The man sees the Good of all he has known merely as Truth. Then his will, his desire, passes into all he knows, and he begins to live his Truth as Good. Truth was first, because it must

49

be. A man must *first* learn Truth. But the Good of Truth is prior to Truth, for all Truth only can come from Good. So Truth is really second to its Good. But in time and space a man must learn everything the wrong way round—we must learn Truth first before we perceive and reach its Good. The man who lay in Truth by the side of the pool of Bethesda put Truth *first* and kept on doing so—and so was always *second*, always too late. He was second because he took Truth as first. Jesus as the realisation of the Good of Truth healed him. The man then put Good first and Truth second and was healed. The miracle is about this deep question of first and second and its reversal. And the reversal makes Good first and Truth second. Then the man is *made whole* because the *wholeness* of Truth lies in the realisation of its Good. The miracle means supremely that a man, however much Truth he knows, cannot act from it with his will unless he sees its Good, and this is the last stage of Truth called the Sabbath, where Good comes first. So he *sins*—being in Truth alone and regarding Truth as first. He misses the mark, taking Truth as an end. He puts Truth first, and not as a means to goodness. So Jesus says to him: "Sin no more." This means in the Greek: "Miss the mark no more." All "sin" (as translated) is, in the Greek, *to miss the mark*, and in this parable or miracle, the missing of the mark, or "sin", refers to putting Truth first and not seeing that it is a means to an end, which is the goodness of Truth and the practice of Truth from the goodness it leads to, and not from itself as mere Truth, as mere doctrine and ritual. For a man who acts only from Truth, from doctrine, from ritual, *sins*—that is, he misses the whole idea of the teaching about inner evolution, about re-birth, about regeneration. He misses the whole point of the Gospels. Consider for a moment all those who, historically, have acted from Truth without goodness. Consider religious history and its horrors and hatreds in this respect. And then think that the real meaning of *sin* is *to miss the mark*. Jesus healed the man at the Pool of Bethesda (which means House of Mercy). When Good comes first a man acts from mercy and grace. Then he is made whole. When he is whole he no longer misses the mark. When Jesus is parting from the man whom he has healed he says to him: "Behold, thou art made whole; sin no more."

To a certain extent everyone asks for Good as when a man puts an extra coal on the fire if it is cold. He does not expect any reward save the Good of the action. But nothing is more difficult to understand than what it means to act from Good in the sense of the Gospels, although the meaning is as practical and non-sentimental as putting on a coal if it is cold. To act from Truth, from knowledge, is easy to grasp. But Truth by itself is merciless and those who act from Truth alone are capable of doing the greatest harm to others.

Let us glance at the Parable of the Good Samaritan which has had perhaps a greater effect on mankind than any of the other parables. It is most known. It can be understood as it stands. In fact, no other parable has passed, as it has, into common knowledge. This parable is about *acting from Good* and not from Truth. A Jew is lying wounded by robbers on the dangerous road between Jerusalem and Jericho. A Jewish priest passes and a Levite passes, and they do not help him. A Samaritan then passes and though the Jews and Samaritans have, on the side of Truth, nothing to do with one another, he stops and binds up the wounds of this injured man. The parable is given after the lawyer, seeking to tempt Christ, has asked him what he should do to inherit eternal life.

"And, behold, a certain lawyer stood up and tempted him, saying, Master, what shall I do to inherit eternal life? And he said unto him, What is written in the law? how readest thou? And he answering said, Thou shalt love the Lord thy God with all thy heart, and with all thy soul, and with all thy strength, and with all thy mind; and thy neighbour as thyself. And he said unto him, Thou hast answered right: this do, and thou shalt live. But he, desiring to justify himself, said unto Jesus, And who is my neighbour? Jesus made answer and said, A certain man was going down from Jerusalem to Jericho; and he fell among robbers, which both stripped him and beat him, and departed, leaving him half dead. And by chance a certain priest was going down that way: and when he saw him, he passed by on the other side. And in like manner a Levite also, when he came to the place, and saw him, passed by on the other side. But a certain Samaritan, as he journeyed, came where he was; and when he saw him, he was moved with compassion, and came to him, and bound up his wounds, pouring

51

on them oil and wine; and he set him on his own beast, and brought him to an inn, and took care of him. And on the morrow he took out two pence, and gave them to the host, and said, Take care of him; and whatsoever thou spendest more, I, when I come again, will repay thee. Which of these three, thinkest thou, proved neighbour unto him that fell among the robbers? And he said, He that shewed mercy on him. And Jesus said unto him, Go, and do thou likewise."

(Luke x, 25–37.)

To act from compassion, to act from mercy, is to act from Good itself and not from any idea of reward. Truth alone has nothing to do with compassion, nothing to do with mercy. The most merciless and atrocious acts have been done in the name of Truth. For Truth divorced from Good has nothing real in it. It has nothing to check it, nothing to unite with it and give it any real being.

§ IV. THE LABOURERS IN THE VINEYARD

On more than one occasion Christ makes use of the phrase: "*Many that are last shall be first and the first last.*" In one place these words are used after the disciples have shewn that their idea of the Kingdom of Heaven is earthly, in accordance with the appearances of things with which they are familiar on earth. Christ has been speaking about how difficult it is for one who is *rich* to enter the Kingdom. He is speaking of being *rich* in contrast to the state of little children who are innocent because they have not yet acquired their false ideas of themselves. The disciples have taken his words literally. Peter exclaims: "Lo, we have left all and followed thee. What shall we have?" And it is exactly this question that all people ask and will always ask who do not yet *understand* anything. *What shall we have?* they demand, as if they had something already, as if they were actually rich. Christ answers his disciples on the level of their comprehension. He promises them that they shall sit on thrones and judge the tribes of Israel. This is said in irony, but the irony is veiled, in view of what he is going to say. He answers: "Verily, I say unto you, that ye which have followed me, in the regeneration, when the Son of Man shall sit on the throne of his glory, ye also shall sit upon twelve thrones, judging the twelve tribes of Israel" (Matt. xix, 28). Then he adds,

52

as if it were an afterthought: "But many shall be last that are first; and first that are last" (Matt. xix, 30). And straightway he goes on to contradict what he has just said to his disciples, owing to the lack of understanding of what the Kingdom is like and what a man must be like to attain it. In the form of a parable he shews them how all earthly ideas of being first, of rewards and of what we call justice, of precedence, are non-existent at that level of understanding which is the Kingdom:

"But many shall be last that are first; and first that are last. For the kingdom of heaven is like unto a man that is a householder, which went out early in the morning to hire labourers into his vineyard. And when he had agreed with the labourers for a penny a day, he sent them into his vineyard. And he went out about the third hour, and saw others standing in the market-place idle; and to them he said, Go ye also into the vineyard, and whatsoever is right I will give you. And they went their way. Again he went out about the sixth and ninth hour, and did likewise. And about the eleventh hour he went out, and found others standing; and he saith unto them, Why stand ye here all the day idle? They say unto him, Because no man hath hired us. He saith unto them, Go ye also into the vineyard. And when even was come, the Lord of the vineyard saith unto his steward, Call the labourers, and pay them their hire, beginning from the last unto the first. And when they came that were hired about the eleventh hour, they received every man a penny. And when the first came, they supposed that they would receive more; and they likewise received every man a penny. And when they received it, they murmured against the householder, saying, These last have spent but one hour, and thou hast made them equal unto us, which have borne the burden of the day and the scorching heat. But he answered and said to one of them, Friend, I do thee no wrong; didst not thou agree with me for a penny? Take up that which is thine, and go thy way; it is my will to give unto this last, even as unto thee. Is it not lawful for me to do what I will with mine own? or is thine eye evil, because I am good? So the last shall be first, and the first last." (Matt. xix, 30–xx, 16.)

This parable is the real answer to Peter's question: "What shall we have?" The Kingdom of Heaven, Christ says, is not as you think, and it is impossible to think concerning it as to what you shall have. It is not something that can be thought of in terms of rewards as men understand them. To think of it as a place where a man shall be given a throne and power and authority over others, as a reward for anything he has given up in this life, is to think of it from ideas that have nothing to do with it. The Kingdom is different from anything on earth, different from anything a man's senses can shew him, different from anything he can think. A new understanding is necessary, born from ideas that Man at the level of "Earth" does not possess. So Christ continually begins by saying that "the Kingdom of Heaven is like unto . . ." And in each parable a new idea is introduced, an idea that no one on earth would naturally possess or could possibly think of for himself. For in passing from the level of understanding technically called "Earth" in the Gospels to the level called "Heaven", the whole basis of a man's thoughts must change. But no one's thoughts can change unless he has new ideas, for he thinks from his ideas. No one can think in a new way with his old ideas. And there can be no *change of mind*, no "repentance", if a man's ideas remain at the level of the "Earth", where his ideas are based on appearances, on things that are seen. To understand anything about the Kingdom, his natural ideas must be left, or rather transcended. For while with his natural ideas he can understand the world and its kingdoms, he cannot understand the higher level of the Kingdom of Heaven. He cannot even begin to understand a single thing about it, for the lower level cannot comprehend the higher.

What is the central idea of the difficult parable of the labourers, that is quite new and strange and does not correspond with our natural ideas? It is the *injustice* of the parable that strikes our level of understanding. According to our standards of thinking those who had worked longer should naturally have a greater reward. And no doubt some of the disciples felt the same, believing that they had been the first called to labour in the vineyard represented by Christ's teaching on earth. The teaching had been first given to the Jews and to the disciples in particular. It was natural for the latter to expect the greatest reward. It was a natural idea. But in order to understand the *psychological meaning* of the parable, the central idea must be grasped, for a parable always contains an idea that is not a natural one, and one which may even contradict any natural idea that we possess. It is easy to understand the disciples' idea of the Kingdom. They had a natural idea of it, derived from life, and Christ knew this and answered them in terms of it when he told them they would sit on thrones and judge others. But the parable he went on to give them cannot be related to any natural idea. Our natural ideas of justice and injustice are amongst the most powerful ideas we have. We are aroused by them more than by anything else. And the human standpoint is presented in the parable in the shape of the labourers who were called first, who expected they would receive more, and murmured against the householder, saying: "These last have spent but one hour and thou hast made them equal unto us which have borne the burden of the day and the scorching heat." The answer is: "Friend, I do thee no wrong; didst thou not agree with me for a penny?" And no doubt they would say: "Yes—but we did not know what would happen. It is gross injustice."

What is the key to that parable? It is found in the passages preceding it, and in the parable itself. It lies in the definition given of the householder into whose vineyard the labourers are called, stage by stage. Who is the householder that is at the head of things? The householder is Good. He is defined as: "*I am good*". The householder says: "Is it not lawful for me to do what I will with mine own? or is thine eye evil because *I am good*?" The whole parable is about acting from the idea of Good and not from the idea of reward. For if a man acts from Good itself, he does not seek a reward for he no longer acts from his self-love or the idea of merit. To act from Good makes all who do so equal. To act from seeing the Good of what one does cannot produce any feeling of rivalry or envy. Nor can it create any feeling that a reward should be expected, for to act from Good is its own reward. And to act from seeing the Good of what one does has nothing to do with length of service or any period of time, for Good is above time. For God is defined as good and God is outside all time. The source of Good is outside time, in eternity. The parable is about eternal values: it is not about time. It has nothing to do with our natural ideas derived from time and eternity. In a passage coming a little earlier, where the rich man comes to Christ and says: "Master, what *good* thing shall I do that I may have eternal life?" The answer is: "Why askest thou me concerning that which is *good*? One there is who is good." Only God is good. No man is good. All goodness, everything that is good, the goodness of anything, whatever it be, is from God. The rich man is rich because he feels he has kept all the commandments. He feels merit. He feels himself justified, and so rich, by acting from *Truth*, by having observed all the commandments: yet perhaps he seems uncertain, for he begins now to ask about Good and how to act from Good. "What good thing shall I do?" So in one account it is said that Jesus looked on him and loved him. Truth is first and Good is last. Then the order is inverted and Good is first and

Truth last, when the man acts from Good. The rich man is told to "sell" all he has and follow Jesus. To act from Good in place of Truth a man must sell all his feeling of merit, all self-evaluation, all sense *that he is good*, all sense that he is first. For if he thinks he is good, he will act from himself, from his self-love, and that is why it is said that only God is good. In Luke it is said: "None is good, save one, even God" (xviii, 19). All good is from God, not from Man. If a man thinks *that he is good* he will inevitably seek a reward for all he does, for he will ascribe good to himself. He will not see good as a force passing into all things. He will feel *he* has acted well; especially if he has given up something in order to do a good action. He will be like Peter who says: "Lo, we have left all and followed thee: what then shall we have?" And in thinking of the parable of the labourers it becomes plain from what follows that the disciples did not understand what it meant, because a few verses later, after the parable had been given and the disciples had listened to it, they became indignant because the mother of the sons of Zebedee comes and asks Jesus if they may sit on his right hand and his left hand in the Kingdom of Heaven. They are still thinking in terms of rewards and power. Christ calls the disciples and says:

> "Ye know that the rulers of the Gentiles lord it over them, and their great ones exercise authority over them. Not so shall it be among you: but whosoever would be great among you shall be your minister; and whosoever would be first among you shall be your servant." (Matt. xx, 25–27.)

And he has already given the explanation of what this means—namely, that if a man begins to act from the Good of what he does and the love of Good itself, he will serve Good and be a servant of Good, and all ideas of authority, place and position, and all ideas of being superior to others, all rivalry, all personal envy and jealousy, and all human ideas of justice and injustice will become non-existent for him. For Good is not a person, and to act from seeing the Good of what one does and taking pleasure in it is to act beyond anything personal.

Chapter Five

THE IDEA OF RIGHTEOUSNESS
IN THE GOSPELS

PART ONE

LET us take some examples from the Gospels of Christ's teaching about what it is necessary to do in order to approach a higher level of Man and at the same time let us find some meaning for one or two phrases used by Christ which are not quite clear. Christ says in one place:

"Except your righteousness shall exceed the righteousness of the scribes and Pharisees, ye shall in no wise enter into the kingdom of heaven." (Matt. v, 20.)

This is a definite statement, having a definite meaning. What does righteousness mean and what does it mean that one's righteousness must *exceed* that of the scribes and Pharisees? The word translated in the above passage as "exceed" implies in the original "being over and above" and so uncommon or remarkable. It is not the *same* kind of righteousness as that of the scribes and Pharisees that must be increased. A man must have another and a remarkable or unusual kind of righteousness over and above this righteousness. Righteousness in its primitive meaning was used of a man who observed the rules or customs of the society he lived in. A man behaved rightly by keeping the laws. Among the Jews righteousness was a matter of the observation of all the minute details of the Levitical law with regard to all its ceremonies, tithes, outer purifications, and so on. This form of external righteousness was many times the subject of attack by Christ. It was false righteousness in terms of what Christ was teaching because it was done "before men". It had no other object than to appear right, outwardly, in the eyes of other people.
Christ said:

"Take heed that ye do not your alms before men, to be seen of them: else ye have no reward with your Father which is in heaven. When therefore thou doest alms, sound not a trumpet before thee, as the hypocrites do in the synagogues and in the streets, that they may have glory of men. Verily, I say unto you, They have received their reward. But when thou doest alms, let not thy left hand know what thy right hand doeth: that thine alms may be in secret: and thy Father which seeth in secret shall recompense thee."

(Matt. vi, 1-4.)

In the above passage Christ is saying that the practice of this form of outer righteousness keeps a man where he is—in his own vanity and self-admiration. Christ is teaching about how a man can evolve—how he can become a New Man. In attacking the form of righteousness belonging to the scribes and Pharisees he is attacking the level of a man where everything he does is for the sake of his own merit and not for its own sake. Such a man justifies himself by outward acts and behaviour. To justify oneself means to make out that one is guiltless. In everyone there is a very complex mental process, continually at work, the object of which is to make a man feel he is in the right, that he is guiltless. Unless he has begun to have any deeper conscience than that of conformity to outer customs and law, of keeping up appearances, or not "losing face", as the term is, it does not matter to him what he really has done. He will justify himself in order that his *external* righteousness may be maintained in the eyes of the world—that is, "before men". This keeps him at a certain level of development. This is why Christ attacks this form of feeling one is in the right. The object of the teaching of the Gospels is that Man should internally evolve and reach a higher level. For this reason it is said that unless a man's righteousness is of a quite different order from that of the scribes and Pharisees he cannot reach this higher level, called the Kingdom of Heaven. Heaven always means this higher inner state or level possible for a man to reach. Remember that the Gospels only speak of an inner evolution possible for Man. The scribes and Pharisees do not mean people who lived long ago but people to-day who are at a certain level, who ascribe merit to themselves in all they do and are charmed by themselves and like themselves above everyone else. They have only "self-love" in their emotional development as distinct from "love of neighbour". All self-love despises others. To appreciate that another has a real existence apart from yourself and what you want is to begin to get beyond the level of emotional development called "self-love".

58

What then does it mean that Man's righteousness must transcend that of the scribes and Pharisees? It will depend upon what a man justifies himself by. It will depend upon what a man seeks to live by—that is, on what order of Truth he seeks to follow. If he only justifies himself in the eyes of the world he will be one kind of man inwardly. The order of Truth taught in the Gospels is different from that of the world and the realities of the senses. There was always a great deal of argument amongst those who heard Christ. In John an example of this is given: "Some said, He is a good man; others said, Not so, but he leadeth the multitude astray." The point is that Christ offended the majority of people who heard him. His words were not only too strange but too strong for them to accept and so they were offended. Everyone is offended when what he justifies himself by is taken away from him. Christ was teaching another order of Truth, another order of what can make a man feel right in himself. He was teaching about the passage from one level of a man to another level of himself. He was speaking all the time about this higher level called the Kingdom of Heaven; but even his disciples thought he was speaking about the world and a kingdom on earth. So when Christ said that a man's righteousness must be something utterly different from that of the scribes and Pharisees, he was speaking of what righteousness means in terms of this higher level and how a man must behave in regard to it. A man, in view of this higher level of himself, could no longer behave in the same way or seek his rewards from the same source and feel himself guiltless by the same means. He had to realise that in view of the Kingdom of Heaven all his self-righteousness was useless and could lead to nothing. When a man receives teaching about inner evolution, he can no longer justify himself as he has done. He can no longer blind himself by his former self-justification to what he really is, in the light of the new order of Truth he has learnt. In the passage quoted above it is said:

> "But when thou doest alms, let not thy left hand know what thy right hand doeth."

This is spoken in reference to this other kind of righteousness through which entry to the Kingdom of Heaven is only possible. What does it mean? In the previous verse it is emphasised that a person must not do his alms "to be seen of men" as do the scribes and Pharisees. Alms signify what you do out of mercy.

This does not mean only charitable acts; it means inner forgiveness, inner can-
celling of debts against others. In the ancient language of parables the left hand
denotes evil and the right hand good. In the Parable of the Separation of the
Sheep from the Goats, at the consummation of the age (not the end of the world),
it is said that the sheep are set on the right hand and the goats on the left. In the
above passage not "letting the left hand know what the right hand doeth" refers
to two levels in Man which must be made distinct. Notice that you must not let
the *left* hand know what the right does, not the other way round. Man at his
ordinary level is "evil", and here it means a man sunk in his own self-love and
vanity, and a creature of the senses. The senses are the world. The right hand means
a higher or the beginning of a higher level of understanding. He must not mix
these two levels—that is, he must not let his left hand know what his right hand
does. The left hand is the lower level dominated by self-love. What a man does
from a higher level must be kept away from a lower level. In acts of inner mercy,
in doing his alms, a man must not act from the idea of reward for to do so is to
act from the level in him called "the scribes and Pharisees"—the level of the world
—the lower level. He must act beyond this level, for the sake of doing good, and
not let what he has done in this respect become a matter of praise and so nourish his
vanity and self-love and self-righteousness. But more than this, he must not even
think about what he has done or converse with himself about it and congratulate
himself on his noble behaviour, otherwise what he has done will pass into meritoriousness, even although no one knows about it. It will drop down to that level
in himself. He will begin to congratulate himself, to fall back, as it were, on his
merit. He must know what it means to keep silence—*in himself*. He must not talk
to himself of what he has done. But, as a rule, when a man does good of any kind,
he longs that others should know it and so he cannot keep silence either in himself,
or in regard to others. He acts before an audience, both internal and external.
Christ speaks first of not acting before an *external* audience and then about not
acting before an *internal* audience, called here the "left hand"—which is the lower
level or life-level in him. Once we understand that everything said in the Gospels
is about reaching a higher, and a possible, level in a man, the meaning of left and
right becomes clear. Left is the lower level and right the higher level. A man on the
lower level, acting from the left hand, feels merit and wishes to justify himself
by his charitable actions and have his reward. This is *one form of righteousness*. But

a man beginning to behave from a higher level, from the right hand, seeks no reward, for he acts from what he sees internally is good and for the sake of what is good itself, so, seeking no reward either from within or without, comes into a righteousness over and above that of "the scribes and Pharisees". He does not speak to others of what he has done, nor does he tell himself how well he behaved. Both towards the outer audience and the inner he is silent. This is what is meant by the phrase "unless your righteousness shall *exceed* that of the scribes and Pharisees ye shall in no wise enter into the Kingdom of Heaven". If a man's righteousness does not *exceed* in this respect, he is kept on a lower level of himself inevitably. This teaching, seen in the light of the lower and higher levels in a man, becomes practical in its meaning as does also the significance of left and right hand. And it is also perhaps possible to understand to some extent what is meant that another and a "hidden" reward may come, spoken of in the sentence "and thy Father which seeth in secret shall recompense thee in secret". An extraordinary misunderstanding of the meaning of these words of Christ is found in the Authorised Version where it is said "and thy Father which seeth in secret shall reward thee openly". It is obvious that the scribe who altered the words in transcription had not any idea of their meaning and could not understand any reason for doing "alms" secretly save for external reward and for the sake of feeling meritoriousness and self-satisfaction and so could not refrain from adding that alms done in secret would be rewarded openly.

And perhaps at this point we might try to understand why it is that so often people, not perceiving that the Gospels are about *re-birth* of a higher level of Man, take everything said in them on their own level, and so mix up two orders or levels of truth. To take the Gospels apart from their central idea of re-birth, which means an inner evolution and implies the existence of a higher level, is to understand nothing of their real meaning. People will then only think of justifying themselves in terms of themselves as they are and the world they know, not understanding that another birth of themselves is demanded, a new form of themselves, not simply an increase of what they are already. And in spite of the fact that the Kingdom of Heaven—that is, the highest possible level of a man—is said to be *within*, and to be the object of final attainment, they think that it refers to some state *after death*, in future time, and not to a state attainable or at least to be striven after, *in this life on earth*—a new state of themselves that actually exists as a possibility *now*, as something *above what one is*, like a room on the next floor of this house that is *oneself*, to which so many references are made in the parables. In consequence of this misunderstanding people cannot separate the left hand from the right, and as a result anything they do runs, as it were, into the lower level, and takes a wrong form; and often this is the cause of absurd, distressing or even evil examples of religious life, owing to the ascribing of what is higher to what is lower, and the mixing up of two orders of ideas. It is like an acorn taking to itself all the teaching about an oak-tree and imagining it is an oak-tree as it is.

From all this we can realise that no one can continue to justify himself in the way he has always done and expect to become another and a New Man. His feeling of his own righteousness must change, for as long as he feels that he is righteous *as he is*, he cannot change. His whole idea of what it means to be righteous must change, because it is exactly people's feeling of being righteous, of *being in the right*, that prevents them from changing. They are satisfied with themselves. It is only others who are wrong, not themselves. And it is also their feeling of being already righteous and in the right that determines their special forms of justifying themselves. From this they derive their feeling or worth and merit, and it is just here that they are most easily upset, most easily *offended*. Is anything more easy than being offended and giving offence? This is the human situation. The extraordinarily harsh teaching of the Gospels is to break this feeling of merit and complacency that everyone openly or secretly rests upon, and this is the source of being offended. In the light of the idea of the Kingdom of Heaven, in view of this possible inner evolution, of this higher level, a man must come to realise that he is almost *nothing* as he is, and that all his vanity, merit, conceit, self-esteem, self-liking, self-satisfaction and self-love, and all his imagination of himself, is practically an illusion. It is indeed only possible to understand that harsh teaching of Christ in view of its aim, which is to break up a man's whole psychology, the man as life has made him, the man he regards himself as, and make him think and feel and act in a new way, so that he begins to move towards a higher level, towards another state of himself that exists within him as a possibility. For to pass from one level to another, from the state of an acorn to the state of a tree, everything must be rearranged and altered. All a man's ordinary relations with different sides of himself must alter. The whole setting of his being must change. The whole man must change. For this reason Christ said:

"I came not to bring peace but a sword. For I came to set a man at variance against his father, and the daughter against her mother, and the daughter-in-law against her mother-in-law: and a man's foes shall be those of his own household."
(Matt. x, 34–36.)

This has not an external, a literal meaning. It signifies an internal upheaval, a change in a man's whole psychology, a change in all that in him is "father", "mother", "daughter", "daughter-in-law", "mother-in-law", and so on—in him, *psychologically*. All his relationships to himself must change, and this means that all his ideas about himself and his whole feeling of himself must change. A man's household means all that is in the man himself—not his body but his psychology—the household of all the different sides of *himself*. All the ideas, all the attitudes, that were the "father" or "mother" of his thoughts and views and opinions and all the relationships resulting from them must change in view of the *sword* which is the power of truth of a higher order. Meeting this higher order of truth a man can no longer be at peace with himself as he is. He must think in a new way—and no one can think in a *new* way merely by adding some extra knowledge to what he already thinks. The whole man must change—that is, his whole mind must change, first of all. This parable refers to the starting-point of Christ's teaching, to μετάνοια (μετάνους)—to a man beginning to think beyond how he always thought, to think in an entirely new way about himself and his meaning and his aim. It is not *repentance*, as translated, but *new thinking*, over and above all that he thought before. In the same way, the righteousness that Christ speaks of is over and above and beyond all that a man has justified himself by and regarded as being his righteousness, his idea of being right. It is, indeed, *meta*-righteousness.

PART TWO

THROUGHOUT the Sermon on the Mount Christ is speaking of what connects a man with another order of life and by what means force, or *bliss*, from this higher level can reach him. In the Beatitudes he says in one place: "Blessed are they that hunger and thirst after righteousness for they shall be filled." To be blessed means to attain bliss. It means an actual state that can be attained, and not an abstract

63

merit, a mark in one's favour, in some moral account-book. The word in the original was used by the Greeks to describe the state of the gods. In this passage, to hunger and thirst after righteousness refers to a righteousness different from self-righteousness, which only regards itself and its own object. To find this other righteousness, a man must "lose himself"—that is, his ideas of himself and his value and merit.

Let us study the meaning of a passage referring to this idea—of "losing oneself". It occurs in the description of the incident where Christ wheels round suddenly on Peter, calling him a stumbling-block because he always took what was said in terms of earthly good. Peter mixed up things on different levels. He did not understand the meaning of not letting the left hand know what the right hand is doing. He mixed the Truth of Christ's teaching in his mind with the "things of men". When Christ tells his disciples of his forthcoming death, Peter says: "Far be it from thee, Lord; this shall never be unto thee." Christ then says to him: "Get thee behind me, Satan: thou art a stumbling-block unto me: for thou mindest not the things of God but the things of men." This shews why Peter is called Satan. Here is one of the definitions of what Satan means in the Gospels. It is mixing up different levels in thinking—for to *mind* here means to *think*. Christ then says: "If any man would come after me, let him deny himself, and take up his cross, and follow me. For whosoever would save his life shall lose it: and whosoever shall lose his life for my sake shall find it" (Matt. xvi, 24–25). "Life" here means "Soul" in the original. A man must lose his soul. When it is said that a man must lose his life, something more complicated is meant here than dying physically. In John, Christ says: "Greater love hath no man than this, that a man lay down his life for his friends." But in the original we find "soul", not "life". A man must lay down his soul: and this is the supreme definition of *conscious love*. He must put his friends (literally, in the Greek, those whom he loves) beyond himself or in place of himself. Christ in this passage speaks of what this means in terms of obedience to what he teaches. A servant, he says, obeys his master, not knowing what the master means. But a friend is one who understands and obeys through understanding, so he says: "Ye are my friends." They are his friends if they obey the order of Truth of which Christ spoke. To obey is to act beyond one's own interests, to put something over and above them. A man cannot lose his soul if he only minds the things of men.

The soul in a man can be related to a lower or a higher level. A man must lose his soul in regard to its relationship to a lower level of himself in order to find it at a higher level. It is only by understanding the double meaning of the phrase to "lose the soul" that many sayings about the soul in the Gospels can be understood. Take for example the phrase: "For what shall it profit a man if he shall gain the whole world and forfeit his soul?" By gaining the whole world, by minding only the things of men, he loses his soul, in regard to a possible inner evolution of himself. Remember that everything in the Gospels refers to an inner evolution the result of which is the attainment of the Kingdom of Heaven. The soul of a grub is not at the level of a butterfly and so it must lose its soul to find it again. By remaining a grub it saves its soul as a grub but loses its soul in another sense—that is, it loses the opportunity of transformation, and, by clinging to itself as it is, misses all that belongs to what it can become. And since Man is also capable of transformation or re-birth his soul is double in the same sense. He can keep it and remain as he is, but, by keeping it, he loses it in regard to its real destiny. Or he can lose it by not remaining as he is and then he will find it again at another level of his own inner evolution. Therefore the soul is a potentiality. That is, it is not a fixed thing but is both what a man is and what he may become. In translating the word "soul" by the word "life" as in the above passage: "Greater love hath no man than this, that a man lay down his life for his friends", it is correct if we understand by the word "life" not physical vital life—the life of the body—but the level of himself he is at. Understand that the life of a man is not the outer life of his physical body, but all he thinks and desires and loves. This is a man's life and this is his soul. The soul is the image of the life. But a man can begin to live differently in himself. He can begin to think differently and feel differently and desire differently and love differently. That is, his own relationship to himself can change so that what he went with in his thoughts and consented to in his desires, in short, all that he once thought was true and felt was good, can change. If this happens the man has another relationship to himself, internally. His life in himself then begins to change. As said already, this is what Christ meant when he said: "I came not to bring peace but a sword. For I came to set a man at variance against his father . . . and a man's foes shall be those of his own household." A man who, through the teaching of the *Word*—that is, through another order of Truth belonging to a higher level—begins to think in a new way and feel in a new way and see his aim and meaning in a new way, can no longer consent to all he previously thought and felt and desired and aimed at, for what a man consents to in himself makes his life and this is his soul. His household—that is, himself—must undergo upheaval. He can no longer be at peace with himself. He must lose his former relationship to himself and this means he must lose his soul, for the soul is the man's life as a whole and the man's life is what he is related to in himself, being what he believes as true and right and consents to as desirable—what he serves in himself, what he thinks as right, what he feels as good. So it is possible to realise that to "lay down one's life" means to cease to live as one has lived but to begin to live in another way and that it does not mean to be killed. It means indeed the reverse—*to begin to live*. At the same time, it means that the soul must be *lost*, for otherwise transformation is not possible, understanding that the soul means what a man has attached himself to in mind and desire and hitherto regarded as *himself*. When Christ told his disciples of the sufferings that they would have to endure when they taught the *Word*, he said to them: "In your patience ye shall win your souls." The Greek word for patience means "staying behind" which can be interpreted as not going with one's desires, not going with oneself. By this means a man can lose his soul on one level and find it again at a higher level.

So far we can understand that the soul in a man can be potentially—that is, through its own powers—related to a lower or a higher level of himself. For a man to pass from a lower to a higher level in himself, his soul must change, in what it relates the man himself to. If the man changes his position in himself, so his relation to himself changes and so his soul changes.

From all this we can begin to realise that the *soul* in a man is not something beautiful or ready-made but something that forms itself in him according to his life and that it is really *all his life*, the image of all he has thought and felt and done.

Chapter Six

THE IDEA OF WISDOM IN THE GOSPELS

I N many of the parables and sayings of Christ a word is used which is translated as *wise*. For example, Christ said to his disciples on one occasion: "Be ye wise as serpents and innocent as doves." "Innocent" means "harmless", "not doing any harm", and has not the moral sentimental Western meaning of not knowing anything: it would indeed be impossible to be "wise" and at the same time not know anything. But the word translated as "wise" does not exactly mean "wise" so much as "clever" or practically intelligent. The Greek word is φρόνιμος which meant in its earliest use *being in one's right senses* and so *having presence of mind* or *having one's wits about one*. Christ says in one place: "The children of this world are wiser in their generation than the children of light," and this passage perhaps brings out more clearly than any other the meaning of the word. Worldly people, in their kind, or at their level, are more practical, more shrewd and business-like, more sagacious and knowing, in regard to what they are aiming at, than the "children of light" in regard to what they are aiming at. They have more presence of mind and in dealing with life are not silly or foolish. To know how to do and actually to do the right thing at the right time is to be φρόνιμος. You will remember that the "Steward of Unrighteousness" (wrongly translated as the Unjust Steward) was called "wise"—that is, φρόνιμος—being commended by his lord because he saw what to do in a very difficult situation and acted with great presence of mind.

This word, φρόνιμος, has therefore a strong, bracing, practical meaning. It is used in the Gospels to define the right action of an intelligent man seeking a higher level of himself through inner evolution. Christ talks of those who are useless in this respect. He compares them with salt that has lost its savour and is not even fit for the dunghill: "If the salt have lost its savour, wherewith shall it be seasoned? It is fit neither for the land nor for the dunghill: men cast it out" (Luke xiv, 34, 35). And here the word translated as "have lost its savour" means literally "has been made foolish". The dunghill is life. People who imagine that believing sentimentally in the Gospels is all that is necessary are *foolish*. They are like the "foolish" man who built his house upon the sand, in contrast to the "wise" man, described as φρόνιμος, who built—that is, constructed for himself—his house upon the rock, and "it fell not, for it was founded upon the rock." This means that the man was φρόνιμος because he based himself on the permanent teaching of inner evolution, called the *Word* in the Gospels, and worked to build himself, his own house, the house of *himself*, upon this basis. He *did the Word*. He acted from it. He applied what he understood to his own life. Thus he based himself on the rock of Truth rather than on the shifting sands of life.

Let us consider in this respect the parable of the ten virgins, five of whom were wise, φρόνιμος, and five foolish or silly. This is a parable about reaching a higher level by inner evolution, here called directly the Kingdom of Heaven.

"Then shall the Kingdom of Heaven be likened unto ten virgins, which took their lamps, and went forth to meet the bridegroom. And five of them were wise, and five were foolish. They that were foolish took their lamps, and took no oil with them: but the wise took oil in their vessels with their lamps. While the bridegroom tarried, they all slumbered and slept. And at midnight there was a cry made, Behold the bridegroom, cometh; go ye out to meet him. Then all those virgins arose, and trimmed their lamps. And the foolish said unto the wise, Give us of your oil; for our lamps are gone out. But the wise answered, saying, Not so; lest there be not enough for us and you: but go ye rather to them that sell, and buy for yourselves. And while they went to buy, the bridegroom came; and they that were ready went in with him to the marriage: and the door was shut. Afterward came also the other virgins, saying, Lord, Lord, open to us. But he answered and said, Verily, I say unto you, I know you not. Watch therefore, for ye know neither the day nor the hour wherein the Son of man cometh."

(Matt. xxv, 1–13.)

The wise virgins are distinguished from the foolish virgins by possessing oil in their lamps. Notice that they refuse to give their oil to the others, but tell them to go and buy it in life. All of them had lamps but only half had oil in them and these are called "clever" or "not silly". They are practical. They realised what was necessary in order to reach this higher level called here the bridegroom. What does it mean that they had oil? They are those who, in relation to Christ's teaching,

have understood something that the others have not understood and this is represented by their having oil in their lamps. The parable must be lifted entirely
off its literal meaning. A lamp is to give light. But, psychologically, it means here
something that can give light, not in a physical sense, but in the sense of light as
used in the Gospels—the light that shines in the darkness of the mind, the light of
new understanding coming from the *Word*. Christ came to give light to human
beings who are described as living in darkness on this earth. They live in the light
of the sun, but this is darkness in comparison with this other light comprehended
only by the understanding. Christ called himself the light of the world. He meant
this other light that can fall on the mind and illuminate the understanding. When
a man lives only from his senses and takes the spectacle of outer life, lit up by the
sun, as his sole end, he is in darkness. John says the darkness does not comprehend
the light; the lower does not understand the higher level. When a man becomes
aware that he is internally incomplete and lost, and that the full meaning of his
existence is to undergo a change, an inner evolution, and receives a new understanding about himself and what he has to do, he already begins to see this light,
this real meaning of his creation. The *Word* is about this real meaning, this light.
Christ taught the *Word*, and so is the light. The *Word* is the teaching about the
way to reach a new level where this light is shed, which lies over and above a man,
but at the same time *within him*. Because the Kingdom of Heaven is within a man,
he can only get contact with it internally. The *way* is in himself, not outside. He
can experience flashes of another consciousness, moments of entirely new meaning,
which shew that a higher level exists in him. They are moments of this light. But
to reach this level permanently a man must be taught the *Word* and taught it first
of all externally, via the senses. He must hear it: but this does not mean merely
to hear it literally, but to begin to understand it, to hear it with his mind, to ponder
it, to think of its meaning, to take it into his inner consciousness and to see himself
in the terms of what it teaches. For his mind must slowly be prepared in order to
change because this higher level is different from a lower level and so the thoughts
belonging to a lower level are not of the same order as those of a higher level.
Something new must be formed in his mind to receive "light"—so he must gradually come to "think in a new way" (or "repent" as it is so wrongly translated).
This gradual change in thinking forms the *lamp* in him. It is formed by the teaching
of the *Word*. But the lamp is not enough by itself. It cannot give light alone—but

it is *necessary*, as the first stage of inner evolution. The second stage, in this parable, is the stage of having *oil* in the lamp. This means that what he knows and sees as new Truth must be applied. Christ said: "Everyone that heareth these words of mine and *doeth* them, shall be likened unto a *wise* man . . . and everyone that heareth these words of mine and doeth them not, shall be likened unto a *foolish* man." Here the two words *wise* and *foolish* appear in the same sense as in the parable of the wise and foolish virgins. To act inwardly from the teaching of Christ, to begin to do it, to begin to work from the understanding of its meaning, to begin to use it and apply it to *oneself* practically—this is to be *wise*. This is to use the *Word* intelligently. This is to be practically clever. And this gives oil in the lamp, individually.

But people can accept Truth of this higher order and yet continue to act only from the level of life. They do not internally obey the new Truth, the new knowledge they have learned, which comes from a higher level, but they continue to obey life and its good when it comes to the point. They have lamps but no oil. These are called the *foolish*, who must go and buy oil from those who sell it. This means that they must continue to get the kind of oil gained from meritorious actions in life which is the only kind of Good they value. "Those who sell it" are those who tell you what is meritorious, what will pay best. To act from merit and reward makes one sort of oil. To act from the teaching of the *Word* and its internally understood meaning is to act from a level higher than life, and nothing in outer life will reward you for such actions. The foolish virgins with lamps and no oil are those who are on one level of Truth and knowledge intellectually—a higher level—but *live* and *do* according to another level. They know one thing, and live and do another. These in the very nature of things shut themselves out from the Kingdom of Heaven—that is, from the attainment of this higher level possible to Man which is his real meaning. It is not that the door is shut on them. The door is not shut; they shut the door on themselves. The kind of oil they get from "buying and selling", the oil of merit, is not that required for entry into another level of humanity. So they are said to be "not clever". They are not clever because they do not see that it is to themselves and the kind of people they are that the teaching of Christ applies. They must not merely think in a new way, through the ideas of the *Word*, but must themselves become different kinds of people. They may know and even believe the Truth on a higher level, and at the same time live on

70

another level, not applying the Truth to themselves. This is their problem: their actual lives are not governed by their knowledge. They know one thing and will another thing. In this parable, the wise virgins are those who actually seek to live from their own understanding of what they have been taught and seek the Good of what they have been taught by practising, by applying, from their own wills, the knowledge to themselves. The foolish, on the other hand, knowing the teaching, continue to seek their Good from life, from rewards, from reputation, from being first, getting to higher and higher positions, having better morals than others, being thought well of, from outwardly conforming to laws and social standards, when internally they are quite different and are only restrained by fear. This is the only Good they know and so they must follow it. And since the whole question lies in what a man deems is Good, and because a man acts solely from what he deems is Good, they are told to go to what they deem Good and get at least that kind of oil, for this is all they can do. They are told to go to those who buy and sell this Good. These foolish virgins return. But even so, they find they are shut out, and are told: "Verily, I say unto you, I know you not." They have no idea of acting from a form of Good beyond life, beyond reward in life, for the sake of what they see is Good in the light of a higher teaching of what is Truth and Good. So they shut themselves out because they mix up two different levels of knowledge as two different levels of Good. If you look narrowly at what is meant by "Good" in the Gospels you will see what is meant. To bring down the teaching about higher Man to the level of Man as he is, to follow the idea of what is Good from the basis of life and its rewards, its merits, its values, its insistence on reputation, outer appearances, and so on, is to shut oneself out from the Kingdom of Heaven, because a man beginning to reach the level of the Kingdom of Heaven does Good for no reward in life but from what he sees internally as Good in the light of the Truth of the *Word* taught him. And it is of no use for any of us to pretend that we already know this kind of Good and act from it. We act from life and its Good, however much we know.

To be a Christian a man must will what Christ taught and do it. If he cannot see the Good of what he is taught, he will not act from it. No matter how much knowledge is given and how true it is, he will not act from it unless he sees by his own inner understanding that it is desirable and good and begins to will its existence. A man is not merely his understanding but what he wills from it, and this is what he does, and this is the whole man. The *Word*—that is, the psychological teaching in the Gospels—is to make a man different, first in *thought*, and then in *being*, so that he becomes a New Man. Merely to know about the *Word* and to make one's oil—one's Good—from the advantages, intrigues and merits of life is not to have the oil that belongs to the lamp of Christ. To act from the *Word*, to act from this teaching about inner evolution, this higher state of Man, to begin to do a very few things in the light of Christ's words through seeing what they mean and *liking* the ideas and so being able to *will* them, without any sense of reward, is another matter. One single act done from willing some truth belonging to that order of teaching called the *Word* will lift a man for a moment far beyond his usual level. In such an act there is no question of bargaining, no question of "how much?", no question of "where do I come in?" and no boasting about it afterwards. One such thing done in the purest part of your understanding because you see the necessity and reality and so the Good of it, one such thing done from the inner will, can begin to set in motion something that has hitherto remained silent and motionless. The seed starts to life. The man, as a seed on which the *Word* can fall, begins to awaken. Light enters into his inner darkness. Truth is one thing, the spirit another—and a man must be re-born, from *water* and *spirit*, before he can become a New Man. *Water* is the Truth, the knowledge and teaching about a higher level; and *spirit* is a man's will passing into this knowledge and uniting it with him, through his seeing its Good, its value. No amount of external teaching will bring about this result. A person may have a lamp—but only through his own most intimate will, only through his deepest consent, only through obeying in secret the knowledge that has formed the lamp in him, will he make oil for it. It is just here that everyone is free. It is just here that everyone, through an inner action, can evolve or not evolve.

Chapter Seven

SIMON PETER IN THE GOSPELS

SIMON PETER is one of the few disciples spoken of in some detail in the Gospels. His character is given in clear outline, although this is not apparent unless the inner meaning of all that is said about him is understood. And in this connexion some understanding of the language of parables is necessary.

Peter's name originally was Simon. He and his brother Andrew were the first disciples to be called by Christ. Their calling is described as follows:

"And passing along by the sea of Galilee, he (Jesus) saw Simon and Andrew the brother of Simon casting a net in the sea: for they were fishers. And Jesus said unto them, Come ye after me, and I will make you to become fishers of men. And straightway they left the nets, and followed him."

(Mark i, 16–18.)

I will speak later of the strange phrase "fishers of men". But it can be mentioned here that in the Gospel of Luke the prophecy that they will become "fishers of men" is more strongly emphasised. Here it is related that after they had toiled all night on the sea and caught nothing, Simon was commanded by Christ to let down the nets whereupon they caught "a great multitude of fishes and their nets were breaking". And "Jesus said unto Simon, Fear not; from henceforth thou shalt catch men." It is clear that some analogy exists between fish and men, in the language used in this incident.

The next event recorded in Mark is that Jesus cured Simon's wife's mother. This incident, too trifling as it stands, has another meaning:

"Now Simon's wife's mother lay sick of a fever; and straightway they tell him (Jesus) of her: and he came and took her by the hand, and raised her up; and the fever left her and she ministered unto them." (Mark i, 30–31.)

Everything recorded in the very concentrated account of Christ's teaching has a special meaning. There is not a sentence, not a single word, in the Gospels,

73

that has not meaning totally beyond the literal meaning. You will notice here that Christ "raised her up"—that is, she was lying down—and that then "she ministered unto them". This has its own meaning. "Lying down" is used in the language of parables in the sense of lying prone mentally, as if asleep, and "standing up" in the sense of beginning to awaken, in the mind. We can even guess the nature of the "fever" that Peter's mother-in-law had and what it means that she was cured and began to accept Christ's teaching. But the incident has a still deeper meaning, that has no connexion with Peter's mother-in-law, for mother, father, mother-in-law, father-in-law, wives, husbands, brothers and sisters, and so on, all *psychologically*, in the ancient language of the parables, denote different sides of a man, different affections, different inner relations *in himself to himself*, to different levels of himself. Just in the same way, a new-born baby, or a little child, may, in the language of the parables, stand for something new and precious starting in a man such as new understanding, new feeling or new thinking—something just beginning in him, something that must not be hurt, must not be offended. Remember that the language of parables bases itself on objects, on physical things, in the natural, seen world of the senses, but that its meaning is beyond objects and things, which only *represent* the *psychological* meaning—that is, meaning above the literal level.

It is related in Mark that when the twelve disciples were appointed by Jesus, "Simon he surnamed Peter". Peter in the Greek is πετρος, a rock or stone. In the Gospel of Matthew the naming of Peter is more fully described. Simon has acknowledged Christ as "the Son of the living God", and Christ says to him:

"Thou art Peter, and upon this rock I will build my church; and the gates of Hades shall not prevail against it. I will give unto thee the keys of the kingdom of heaven:" (Matt. xvi, 18, 19.)

Peter is promised the keys of heaven which signifies that he has the power to understand the teaching that Christ was giving to mankind on earth about a possible inner evolution of Man to an inner state called *heaven* as distinct from *earth*. But as yet his power is intellectual, for *rock* or *stone* refers only to *knowledge*—the knowledge of the truth that Christ taught. He is mentally adequate but as yet his belief in Christ is *through* Christ, and not in himself. In this sense he is comparable with the second category defined in the Parable of the Sower, where the man "sown on rocky ground" is described who receives the Word of the Kingdom—

the teaching of a possible inner evolution of Man—with enthusiasm, but has not *root in himself*, so that when tribulation arises, he stumbles. He receives the *Word* intellectually—hence the reference to rocky ground. He receives it as knowledge. And this is also shewn in the fact that when Peter saw Christ, whom he regarded as a king who would establish a kingdom on earth, being led away to the crucifixion, he denied him. He is always shewn as passionate, violent, and undeveloped in his emotions. He had no emotional understanding, though he had apparently an intellectual grasp of the teaching. You must picture him as a hot-tempered enthusiastic man, listening eagerly to everything Christ taught his disciples in private, remembering what was said, impatient of the others, with his whole emotional nature fastened on the *actual visible person* of Christ. He imagined himself capable of an undying loyalty to the person of Christ. He caught his teaching at one level, but did not see as deeply as probably some of the others saw. Hasty, quick, intellectually brilliant, violent, full of self-love, he was a man whom Christ recognised as being capable, after great suffering, to take hold of the teaching eventually *from himself*. Christ saw him as a man at present without *root in himself*, but capable of having a great depth of root after he had been given the shocks to his own nature that were necessary. And the shock of the crucifixion was the greatest shock of all to him—and to the disciples in general. Imagine what they felt when they witnessed Christ led forth to die the lowest kind of death—the death reserved only for criminals. How many of the followers of Christ must have felt there could be no real Truth or meaning in the teaching they had heard if such a fate awaited the teacher. Since Peter could not value the teaching apart from the *person* of the teacher—that is, he had *no root in himself*, but he was outwardly dependent—Christ warns Peter about his inability to attain to the teaching apart from the teacher. This occurs when Christ foretells his death:

"From that time Jesus began to shew unto his disciples, how that he must go into Jerusalem, and suffer many things of the elders and chief priests and scribes, and be killed, and the third day be raised up. And Peter took him, and began to rebuke him, saying, Be it far from thee, Lord: this shall never be unto thee. But he turned and said unto Peter, Get thee behind me, Satan: thou art a stumbling block unto me: for thou mindest not the things of God, but the things of men." (Matt. xvi, 21–23.)

And you must understand that all these incidents concerning Peter have their significance in regard to the kind of man Peter was. In one way he was like Nicodemus who could only believe through the seen miracles and was told by Jesus that the whole thing lay in being re-born *internally* and not in matters belonging to the evidence of the senses. It is true that Peter was cast in bigger mould than Nicodemus but Jesus expressly tells him that he has *no real faith*. He says to Peter:

"Simon, Simon, behold Satan asked to have you, that he might sift you as wheat: but I made supplication for thee, that thy faith fail not: and do thou, when once thou hast turned, stablish thy brethren. And he said unto him, Lord, with thee I am ready to go both to prison and to death. And he said, I tell thee, Peter, the cock shall not crow this day, until thou shalt thrice deny that thou knowest me." (Luke xxii, 31–34.)

In the Gospel of John the incident is related differently:

"Simon Peter saith unto him, Lord, whither goest thou? Jesus answered, Whither I go, thou canst not follow me now; but thou shalt follow afterwards. Peter saith unto him, Lord, why cannot I follow thee even now? I will lay down my life for thee. Jesus answereth, Wilt thou lay down thy life for me? Verily, verily, I say unto thee, The cock shall not crow, till thou hast denied me thrice." (John xiii, 36–38.)

Here Christ foretells the change in Peter when he says: "thou shalt follow me afterwards". The cock signifies awakening, and *thrice* means denial in the full extreme. Peter would not awaken until his own self-feeling about Christ was destroyed. When he realised how fully he could deny Christ he awoke. The cock crew. It is said in Luke that Peter "wept bitterly" when the cock crew and Christ turned and "looked upon him". He wept because the teaching of Christ became at that moment emotional in him. He saw himself in the light of the knowledge he had been taught. He saw the distance that lay between what he knew and what he was. In place of merely knowing he began to *understand*. But before this happened to Peter he believed only through Christ, and as long as a man believes through another man he has no *faith* for he believes through his senses and not through his inner understanding—that is, the root is not *in himself*. If things go badly, he ceases to believe. And a man who believed as did Peter, before his emotional regeneration, can only prevent others believing. To believe passionately, violently, in someone prevents others from understanding. Such a person uses his Truth, his knowledge of Truth, violently, and as it were cuts off another person's understanding. This happens because the emotional state of the man who has only Truth and knowledge is wrong. He is a partisan. There is no patience in him. This is one meaning of the incident where Peter cuts off the ear of the high priest's servant:

> "Simon Peter, therefore having a sword, drew it, and struck the high priest's servant, and cut off his right ear . . . Jesus therefore said unto Peter, Put up the sword into the sheath." (John xviii, 10, 11.)

In another Gospel it is said that Christ "touched his ear and healed him" (Luke xxii, 51). *Sword* means Truth fighting, and the *ear* is always used as the emotional understanding in the Gospels, as in "Blessed are those who have ears to hear", etc., where "ears" means, psychologically, the power of emotional hearing. Jesus rebuked Peter and told him to put up the sword, and restored the man's ear. All this has a meaning totally apart from its literal *sense-based* meaning; and in order to understand such things, you must get away entirely from the historical narrative and the actual picture of the events unrolled in the description. The historical description is made to represent the psychological meaning, not the other way round. *The whole drama of Christ represents another meaning* and the fitting together of the historical narrative is done in view of the psychological meaning. But it is for a long time difficult to escape from the literal, natural mind in regard to such matters and to open up another level of understanding.

Peter is the violent man of knowledge, in this case the man who is taught the Truth of the possible inner evolution of Man and receives it only as knowledge and thinks from its logic. And there is nothing more merciless than the logic of Truth alone. All the persecutions in the Church were from *Truth alone*, from some disputed detail of knowledge, without mercy. When a man thinks intellectually, he thinks logically; emotional thinking is psychological. A man who thinks logically has no mercy, for he has no understanding. He is the man of dogma. In science, he is the man who uses his science for murder. Yet remember that Christ taught that love of God and love of neighbour is the whole formulation of his teaching. He said:

77

"Thou shalt love the Lord thy God with all thy heart, and with all thy soul, and with all thy mind. This is the first and great commandment. And a second like unto it is this, Thou shalt love thy neighbour as thyself. On these two commandments hangeth the whole law, and the prophets."

(Matt. xxii, 37–40.)

Because Peter was a man of knowledge and not yet emotionally awake, he could not forgive. To forgive comes from emotional development. Only through emotional development can we cancel the debts of others. All emotional development means to develop beyond self-love and all its absorbing interests, to the stage of "love of neighbour". It is typical of Peter to ask Christ: "Lord, how oft shall my brother sin against me, and I forgive him? until seven times?" Jesus answers him: "I say not unto thee, Until seven times; but, Until seventy times seven." Then he addresses the following parable directly to Peter:

"Therefore is the kingdom of heaven likened unto a certain king, which would make a reckoning with his servants. And when he had begun to reckon, one was brought unto him, which owed him ten thousand talents. But forasmuch as he had not wherewith to pay, his lord commanded him to be sold, and his wife, and children and all that he had, and payment to be made. The servant therefore fell down and worshipped him, saying, Lord, have patience with me, and I will pay thee all. And the lord of that servant, being moved with compassion, released him, and forgave him the debt. But that servant went out, and found one of his fellow-servants, which owed him a hundred pence: and he laid hold on him, and took him by the throat, saying, Pay what thou owest. So his fellow-servant fell down and besought him, saying, Have patience with me, and I will pay thee. And he would not: but went and cast him into prison, till he should pay that which was due. So when his fellow-servants saw what was done, they were exceedingly sorry, and came and told their lord all that was done. Then his lord called him unto him, and saith unto him, Thou wicked servant, I forgave thee all that debt, because thou besoughtest me: shouldest thou not also have had mercy on thy fellow-servant, even as I had mercy on thee? And his lord was wroth, and delivered him to the tormenters, till he should pay all that was due. So shall also my heavenly Father do unto you, if ye forgive not every one his brother from your hearts." (Matt. xviii, 23–35.)

To forgive must come from the heart. It is emotional.

When a man has the love of goodness in him he does not judge from the love of Truth alone. The man of Truth is morose and gloomy. He sees everything logically. And Truth alone judges us all and condemns us all. Only mercy can find a way out, and that mercy must begin with others: "Forgive us as we forgive others", as it is said in the Lord's Prayer.

Peter was a violent man emotionally. His emotions were mechanical emotions. Mechanical love and conscious love are very different. In life people love mechanically. This mechanical love can easily turn to hate and so to denial. Conscious love cannot. Through mechanical love we all suffer: conscious love heals us. Peter's love for Christ was mechanical love, not conscious love. Therefore Christ tried to shew him the nature of love. In the passage which I am now going to quote two different words are used in the Greek to express the two different kinds of love, mechanical love and conscious love, but in the translation no distinction has been made and the word "love" is used to represent both the Greek φιλέω and the Greek ἀγαπαω. In speaking to Peter Christ twice uses the word ἀγαπαω expressing conscious love, but Peter uses the word φιλέω which refers to ordinary mechanical love. In quoting the incident I will emphasise the distinction by altering the translation:

> "Jesus saith to Simon Peter, Simon, son of John, lovest thou me (consciously) more than these? He saith unto him, Yea, Lord, thou knowest that I love thee (mechanically). He saith unto him, Feed my lambs. He saith unto him again a second time, Simon, son of John, lovest thou me (consciously)? He saith unto him Yea, Lord, thou knowest that I love thee (mechanically). He saith unto him, Tend my sheep. He saith unto him the third time, Simon, son of John, lovest thou me (mechanically)? Peter was grieved because he said unto him the third time, Lovest thou me (mechanically)? And he said unto him, Lord, thou knowest all things, thou knowest that I love thee (mechanically). Jesus said unto him, Feed my sheep." (John xxi, 15–17.)

Peter could not understand what Christ meant.

An earlier incident relates how Peter walked on the waters and began to sink. This is described in Matthew. The disciples were in their boat in a storm and saw Jesus walking on the water towards them and were afraid.

"But straightway Jesus spoke unto them, saying, Be of good cheer; it is I; be not afraid. And Peter answered him and said, Lord, if it be thou, bid me come to thee upon the waters. And he said, Come. And Peter went down from the boat, and walked upon the waters, to come to Jesus. But when he saw the wind, he was afraid; and beginning to sink, he cried out, saying, Lord, save me. And immediately Jesus stretched forth his hand, and took hold of him and saith unto him, O thou of little faith, wherefore didst thou doubt?"

(Matt. xiv, 27–31.)

It is clear that this passage means, in its deeper, non-literal sense, that Peter had little or no faith. The origin of faith is from seeing internally the truth of a thing, independently of any corroboration afforded by the evidence of the external senses. Peter believed through the visible person of Christ and not from anything in himself. The teaching given him by Christ was not yet something distinct from the visible Christ towards whom he felt such passion of loyalty, and so it had not reached that level *in himself* technically termed *faith*. Faith is not blind belief, but seeing for oneself the truth of a thing. And faith is not believing from the senses. The kind of Truth that Peter had was not strong enough to support him, for its origin was not in him but outside him, in the person of his teacher. So his Truth, not being of the order of faith, could not support him. Water, in the language of parables, refers to a certain kind of Truth—not Truth in general or the source of Truth. Moses struck water out of the rock. Water is Truth related to Man, in a form that represents the Truth or knowledge about himself in connexion with inner evolution or re-birth. But as such it is not living—that is, is not "living water". *Faith* makes such Truth living: or rather, it is the starting point for *faith* abstracted from sense and builds itself on another side or in another part of a man, distinct from the side or part governed by the limited external instruments of sense. The knowledge, the Truth, in Peter, was still wrongly based. He did not see its inner meaning, having always his eyes eagerly fastened on the outer Christ—the beloved Christ that his senses revealed. When he sought to trust himself to this kind of truth, he failed. Such truth did not *support* him save for a moment, and so he is told that he had no faith. He did not really understand the meaning of all that he had been taught, as yet. That came later. He tried to walk on the basis of his truth and, sinking, had to cry out for the support of

Christ. The external world had more power over him than the internal—that is, external meaning had more power than internal meaning. For this reason it could not hold him up. Immediately difficulties arose, immediately the winds blew and the waves rose, he lost sight of it and began to sink. And all this means that *internally*—in himself—life and the teaching of Christ were mixed up and not yet separated out. For we can see, from the flexible transitions that belong to the deep language of parables, in view of a remark of Christ that his teaching is not of this world, that Peter could not yet, through the order of Truth taught by Christ, walk above the Truth belonging to life.

The change in Peter's emotional development is shown in the final incident concerning him after the resurrection of Christ. It is related that Peter said to the other disciples: "I go a fishing". Some of the other disciples went with him and they fished all night but caught nothing.

"But when day was now breaking, Jesus stood on the beach: howbeit the disciples knew not that it was Jesus. Jesus therefore saith unto them, Children, have ye aught to eat? They answered him, No. And he said unto them, Cast the net on the right side of the boat, and ye shall find. They cast therefore, and now they were not able to draw it for the multitude of fishes. That disciple therefore whom Jesus loved saith unto Peter, It is the Lord. So when Simon Peter heard that it was the Lord, he girt his coat about him (for he was naked), and cast himself into the sea. But the other disciples came in the little boat (for they were not far from the land, but about two hundred cubits off), dragging the net full of fishes. So when they got out upon the land, they see a fire of coals there, and fish laid thereon, and bread. Jesus saith unto them, Bring of the fish which ye have now taken. Simon Peter therefore went up, and drew the net to land, full of fishes, a hundred and fifty and three: and for all there were so many, the net was not rent. Jesus saith unto them, Come and break your fast. And none of the disciples durst enquire of him, Who art thou? knowing that it was the Lord. And Jesus cometh and taketh the bread, and giveth them, and the fish likewise." (John xxi, 4–13.)

This incident contains many ideas. Behind its outer form lie many meanings. To take it literally is to take it on one level only. Can you suppose that precisely one hundred and fifty-three fish were caught? Can you suppose that the record that Peter was naked and then girt his coat about him before he cast himself into the sea is to be taken literally? Why record such a trivial and, at the same time, such a curious incident? Peter had denied Christ, having only belief, and so being stripped of faith, so he is shewn here as naked. The "armour of faith"—the covering to the mind that enables a man to think clearly beyond the senses and to live untouched by the events of the world, and stand fast in another interpretation of life—was lacking. So Peter was naked. But hearing from John that Christ was present he seized the coat of faith he had discarded and approached Christ again. But the general meaning in regard to Peter is that he became able to catch men, after he had been helped. In the earlier Greek Orphic religious teaching, a similar idea of Man being a fish to be caught and lifted out of the ocean is found. The sun, for example, is represented as fishing for Man.

Behind all the rising and setting external forms of religion in the world there has been a broad, fully-developed stream of knowledge, always the same and always having the same object—namely, the inner quickening and inner growth and evolution of Man to a higher level of himself. So similar ideas outcrop at widely separated historical periods, coming from this source. Centuries later, in the legend of the Holy Grail, said to have been the cup in which Christ's blood was caught by Joseph of Arimathaea, the *fisher-king* appears. To catch men from the sea is to lift them out of the service of nature, to bring them to the realisation of another more conscious world in which they must learn to breathe, by means of another order of Truth. Peter had become a fisher of men. He fulfilled Christ's prediction: "From henceforth thou shalt catch men." (Luke v, 10.)

Chapter Eight

THE IDEA OF PRAYER

INTRODUCTION

SO many references are made to prayer in the Gospels that it is useful to collect some of them together and try to gain an idea of what was taught by Christ about the meaning of prayer and the conditions necessary for it to obtain any response. Prayer is directed to what is above a man—to what is at a higher level than himself. We have already seen that the language of parables, as used in the Gospels, conveys meaning from a higher to a lower level. Prayer is conveying meaning from a lower to a higher level. The one is heaven communicating with earth, and the other earth trying to communicate with heaven. And since we have also seen that there is a difficulty in the communicating of the higher with the lower, we shall not be surprised to find that there is a similar difficulty in the communicating of the lower with the higher. The two levels are not in contact.

Let us again remind ourselves that the central *conception of Man* in the Gospels is that he is an unfinished creation capable of reaching a higher level by a definite evolution which must begin by his own efforts, and that their entire teaching is about what must be done for this to be effected. In this light the Gospels are nothing but a series of instructions that concern a possible and definite pre-established psychological development that Man is capable of, and one that, if he begins to set himself to the task of its fulfilment, opens his eyes and makes him see in which direction his full meaning lies. And let us also remind ourselves that the attainment of this higher level possible for Man is called *heaven* or the *Kingdom of Heaven* in the Gospels and that it is *within* a man, as a possibility of his own inner evolution or re-birth of himself, and that Man at the level he is on, as an unawakened creature, an unfinished experiment, is called *earth*. These are the two levels, the higher and the lower, and some very great differences exist between them, as great as the differences between a seed and a flower. Thus

83

communication between these two levels is difficult. The mission of Christ was to bridge, to connect, and to bring into correspondence in himself these two levels, the divine and human; and of this we will speak in another place. But it can be said here that unless this connection is made by a few at certain intervals in time, all communication with the higher fails and Man is left without any ideas or teachings that can lift him—that is, he is left to his instincts, his self-interests, his violence and his animal appetites, and so without any influences that can lift him beyond the level of barbarism.

THE NECESSITY OF PERSISTENCE IN PRAYER

In view of the difficulty of communication between the lower and the higher level, it is possible to understand that direct contact with *God* is not easy, as religious people often believe. Religious people often think that they can come in contact with a higher level—that is, with *God*, just as they are. They do not realise that for this to be possible they must become different. Let us now look at some of the observations made about prayer in the Gospels in connexion with the idea that *persistence* is necessary. One of Christ's disciples asks how to pray. He says: "Lord teach us how to pray even as John taught also his disciples." (There is, by the way, no record of how John taught his disciples to pray.) Christ says in reply:

"When ye pray, say, Father, Hallowed be thy name. Thy kingdom come. Give us day by day our daily bread. And forgive us our sins; for we ourselves also forgive everyone that is indebted to us. And bring us not into temptation."

(Luke xi, 2–4.)

Notice how Christ goes on. He says:

"Which of you shall have a friend, and shall go unto him at midnight, and say unto him, Friend, lend me three loaves; for a friend of mine is come to me from a journey, and I have nothing to set before him; and he from within shall answer and say, Trouble me not: the door is now shut, and my children are with me in bed; I cannot rise and give thee? I say unto you, Though he

84

will not rise and give him because he is his friend, yet because of his importunity he will arise and give him as many as he needeth." (Luke xi, 5–8.)

Christ emphasises that persistence is necessary and uses an illustration that seems to suggest that it is as if prayer is addressed to someone who hears but does not wish to be bothered and is forced to do something only if there is sufficient persistence; and Christ indicates that it is through shameless persistence that a response is obtained. The word translated as "importunity" means, literally, shameless impudence. The same idea, namely, that prayer is not easily answered, is expressed in another passage:

"And he spake a parable unto them that they ought always to pray and not to faint; saying, There was in a city a judge, which feared not God, and regarded not man: and there was a widow in that city; and she came oft unto him, saying, Avenge me of mine adversary. And he would not for a while: but afterward he said within himself, Though I fear not God, nor regard man; yet because this widow troubleth me, I will avenge her, lest she wear me out by her continual coming." (Luke xviii, 1–5.)

A parallel is drawn between the widow who asks for justice from a judge who acts only because he is forced, in order to save himself trouble, and the man who prays to God. All this means that prayer is not easily answered. Barriers exist. Help is not easily obtained. Christ tells his disciples in many places to pray continually, but he does not tell them that prayer is easily answered. It is not an easy matter to obtain response from a higher level to requests coming from a lower level. Only persistence and intensity can cause the higher level to respond. The difficulty is shewn as being like the difficulty of prevailing upon a man in bed to get up, or a worldly judge to render justice to a widow. Christ taught that in regard to prayer and getting help for it, matters are just as they are on earth, as when a man asks for help from people who are reluctant to give it. But in the case of prayer, it is not actually a question of reluctance, but a difficulty inherent in the nature of things. What is lower is not in contact with what is higher. Understand this point clearly: the lower is not in direct contact with the higher. God and Man are not on the same level. The whole conception of the invisible aspect of the Universe or spiritual world implicit in the teaching of the Gospels is that there are higher and lower levels distinct from one another and that it is arranged in an order of what is *above* and what is *below*—that is, in levels. The lower is not in direct touch with the higher, as the ground-floor of a house is not in direct touch with the top floor. And so, to reach what is above, many difficulties stand in the way, which makes it look as if there were reluctance on the part of the higher level to respond to the lower. It is not a question of reluctance, but it seems like it to the human mind and so is illustrated in such terms by Christ in the above comparisons, which shew that great effort is necessary in order to obtain any response to prayer. It is as if a man who prayed in earnest had to throw something up to a *certain height* by an intensity of purpose before he could expect to make anyone hear or get any response, and, failing to do so, failing to make the request rightly, failing to throw it up to a high enough level, thought he was praying in vain, to someone who was reluctant to do anything, and so began to be faint-hearted. He must insist. A man's prayer, his aim, his request, must be persisted in; it must go on, in spite of not being answered. He must have *shameless impudence*. As Christ says, "he must pray continually and not faint". This expression "not faint" means in the original "not behave badly". He must pray continually and not behave badly in regard to all the difficulties connected with praying.

THE NECESSITY OF SINCERITY IN PRAYER

Christ speaks sometimes of the attitude from which a man prays. It is useless to pray from a wrong attitude and so a man must look into himself and see from what in himself he prays because no communication with a higher level is possible through what is insincere and false in him. Only what is sincere and genuine in him can touch a higher level. For example, any trace of *vanity* or *self-conceit* or *arrogance* stops communication with a higher level. That is why so much is said about the *purification of the emotions* in the Gospels; for the greatest *impurity* in a man and the one most constantly pointed out in the parables and sayings of Christ comes from the feelings of self-righteousness, self-excellence, self-merit and superiority, and so on. This is shewn in the following parable which is addressed to "certain which trusted in themselves that they were righteous, and set all others at nought":

"Two men went up into the temple to pray; the one a Pharisee, and the other a publican. The Pharisee stood and prayed thus with himself, God, I thank thee, that I am not as the rest of men, extortioners, unjust, adulterers, or even as this publican. I fast twice in the week; I give tithes of all that I get. But the publican, standing afar off, would not lift up so much as his eyes unto heaven, but smote his breast, saying, God, be merciful to me a sinner. I say unto you, This man went down to his house justified rather than the other: for every one that exalteth himself shall be humbled; but he that humbleth himself shall be exalted."   (Luke xviii, 10–14.)

To pray—to enter into touch with a higher level—a man must know and feel he is *nothing*, in comparison with what is above him. But he must truly see that this is so, and not merely feel it as by looking at the stars a man feels how small the earth is. This is feeling small by physical magnitude: a man must feel small through psychological magnitude. Unless a man feels he is nothing prayer is useless, in just as practical a sense as a match is useless if wet. A man is pure in his emotional life in proportion as he feels his own nothingness, his own ignorance, and his own helplessness. And exactly the same idea is expressed by Christ when he speaks of doing things from oneself and not from one's vanity:

"And when ye pray, ye shall not be as the hypocrites: for they love to stand and pray in the synagogues and in the corners of the streets, that they may be seen of men. Verily, I say unto you, They have received their reward. But thou, when thou prayest, enter into thine inner chamber, and having shut thy door, pray to thy Father which is in secret, and thy Father which seeth in secret shall recompense thee."   (Matt. vi, 5, 6.)

To enter into "thine inner chamber and shut the door" means to go right into the house of yourself, into the innermost room, and, shutting the door on everything outer, to pray from that inner self that is not a servant of the public or an invented social myth or a seeker of rewards and success and outer praise. It is to pass beyond all connexion with vanity or self-conceit. It is only the *internal Man* in a man that can obtain response to prayer and can communicate with a higher level. The external worldly side of a man, the pretending man, cannot pray.

87

All these instructions and many similar ones are about *how to transmit messages to a higher level*. They are practical instructions in the method of transmission, of telepathy, which is only possible through *real* emotions. Only real emotions can transmit; only real emotions are telepathic. False emotions based on vanity and self-conceit cannot transmit. To get a response to prayer, prayer must be of a certain quality. It must fulfil certain conditions, and one is that it must originate from an absolutely pure and genuine emotional feeling, otherwise it cannot reach its goal. So a man must purify himself from self, in his emotional life, and this means he must develop emotionally. That is, he must begin to love his neighbour. This is the first stage of emotional development taught by Christ. And how difficult it is. How difficult it is to behave consciously to others—even to those one imagines one loves already. Can you say you love beyond your self-love? It is only the emotions that lie beyond the self-love and the self-emotions that can communicate with anything beyond oneself. And, after all, this might be expected—once we come to think about the question. How can self-emotions communicate with other people? They communicate only with oneself. So you see why "love of neighbour" is insisted upon.

RESPONSE TO PRAYER

In connexion with praying, Christ says: "Ask and ye shall receive". But a man must know what to *ask* means. Prayer is the means of getting a response from a higher level of the Universe so that its influences come down and enter momentarily into what is at a lower level. Let us consider what to *ask* means. Seen aright, the Universe is *response to request*. The scientist works confidently, believing that he will get a *response* from the physical Universe as a result of his experiments, theories and efforts, which form his *request*. This is *prayer* in one form. He gets a response if he finds the right way to *ask*, and this means if his request takes the right form. But to find the right form of request takes time, trouble and effort, and not only "shameless impudence" but also the feeling of certainty in the unknown—that is, faith. For example, the scientist, by his persistent requests, has discovered and brought into communication with human life the forces of electricity and electro-magnetics in general which belong to another world—an

infra-world, the world of electrons. This is response to request. This is communication, in one sense, with another world. Now we perceive that we live in
a ready-made Universe of great complexity very far beyond our comprehension
but we are sure that it will respond to our efforts. This is indeed our attitude to
the Universe and one that we do not question. We are sure that if we try to
find out how to make something, we shall be given a result. When you cook
food you get a response exactly according to the form of your request. If the results
are not what you expected, you are getting a wrong response, not because the
Universe is at fault but because the form of your request is wrong. You do not
know how to *ask* rightly and so must learn how to cook better—that is, how to
ask better. To ask is to request. If we did not live in a Universe, visible and
invisible, that gives a *response to right request* (whatever the nature of that response,
good or evil), neither the scientist nor the man who prays for inner help could
expect to obtain any response. Nevertheless to obtain a response is not always
easy. Certain conditions must be fulfilled. In regard to prayer as request or asking,
it must not be mechanical or mere matter of repetition, of thinking that "much
speaking" will give a result; it is not the quantity but the *quality* of prayer that
is important. The mere repetition of words is unavailing. Christ said: "*In praying
use not vain repetitions*". And, as we have already seen, prayer must be persisted in.
A man must have some idea about what he is asking for, and must persist in his
request and believe that it is possible to obtain a result. And just as a scientist, in
his particular mode of prayer to the natural Universe, makes a request once he
has the idea that he can discover something and feels it is possible, and modifies
again and again his request by trial and error and by ingenuity, until he obtains
a response through finding the right request, so a man who prays to the spiritual
Universe must have the same faith, patience, intelligence and power of inventive-
ness. A man must work and labour and invent in regard to his own development
as much as the scientist must in regard to making a new discovery. The scientist
will get a response if things are right as regards the request, and so will the man
who prays if his request is right for himself. But he must know himself and
understand what to request. To *ask* something that is impossible or to ask what
will only harm oneself is to ask wrongly.

REQUEST IN PRAYER

What are we to ask for in prayer? In the prayer that Christ formulated for his disciples when they asked him how to pray, all ordinary personal wishes are apparently ruled out. But since everything said in the Gospels is about reaching the higher level of inner evolution possible for Man, called the Kingdom of Heaven, it is not surprising that it has a non-earthly quality. Yet in view of its object it could not be more personal. The Lord's Prayer is about self-evolution. The opening phrase marks the higher level: "Father, Hallowed be thy name, Thy kingdom come". That is, may communication be established between the higher and lower. A connexion between earth and heaven is asked for. This is the first request, and you will understand that this means reaching a definite emotional state for these words to be said with any intensity of meaning. In other versions it is "Our Father in Heaven". A man might well spend a minute, an hour, or a life-time, before he reached the emotional perception of the meaning of these opening words which must be said consciously. Then comes the request for daily bread, which does not mean literal bread but "trans-substantial" bread. The meaning of the original word is unknown, but its intention is "spiritual" bread or food that nourishes the understanding of a man in the struggle to raise himself to a higher level. Then comes the request to be forgiven, as we forgive others; and this means that to reach a higher level it is absolutely necessary first of all to cancel the debts of others recorded in that account-book we all keep in our memories of what we imagine we are owed by the bad behaviour of others to us and their lack of consideration to ourselves. Not to forgive others is to keep oneself held down and chained to the "earth". We imprison ourselves, fasten ourselves down, keep ourselves where we are, if we cannot cancel debts, and as we forgive others so we are forgiven for our innumerable mistakes, failures in the growth of our own understanding—that is, in our own evolution. Then comes the strange request not to be brought into temptation. But let us realise that no man can undergo inner evolution and a development of understanding without temptation and that the nature of this kind of temptation is different from what people usually regard as temptation, which they associate with the flesh and its weaknesses. For example, we are always being tempted to misunderstand or understand wrongly. When a man sets himself on the path of development indicated in the Gospels he becomes tempted by all sorts of doubts and disbeliefs and extraordinary inner difficulties of understanding which he must pass through, where his *human* reasoning powers based on the evidence of the senses fail him completely and only the certainty that *there is something*, only the conviction that the path he is on leads *somewhere*, in short, only his *faith*, can assist him. For faith means not only *certainty* beyond any sense-based proof but a conviction of possibilities before one has realised them: and so Christ says in one place: "All things whatsoever ye pray for and ask for, have faith that ye *have* received them, and ye *shall have* them." Notice then that you must have a thing before you receive it; you must act as if you have what you as yet have not, and you shall have it. This seems very strange; but everything that has to do with establishing connexion with a higher level and all instructions concerning the nature of the effort required seem strange. Consider—would not a seed think instructions about becoming a flower strange? To pass from one level to even the first beginnings of another level is to pass through very difficult temptations of which no one, who is content with himself as he is, has any idea. But the key to understanding the Lord's Prayer lies in the opening phrase. It is prayer about reaching a higher level. "May thy kingdom come": May I come into thy kingdom: May the will of heaven, of a higher level, be done on me as earth. And the last request not to be tempted too much, beyond one's strength, concerns that endeavour, for many things stand in the way, and, as it is put in the allegories of the Old Testament, God wrestles with Man and seeks to overcome and even slay him. This is how the struggle to lift oneself off the level one is at, up to a new level, is expressed. It is as if this very thing one prays for and wishes becomes an enemy, opposing every step made. But if we remember that the reaching of a higher level means a transformation and re-birth of oneself, the idea becomes plain. A man *as he is* cannot reach a higher level. He cannot approach God as he is. The higher level is bound to oppose him as long as he remains the same kind of man.

Now all these requests are about reaching another state. The Lord's Prayer is wholly about this goal. It is not about life. It shews, in brief, apart from all else said in the parables and teaching about the same thing, that the meaning of prayer, essentially, is to reach a higher level, and that all prayer should be about this; and that a man, in praying, should think primarily of this, and request more than all else what is necessary for this to be attained. For this is the supreme *aim*. Christ defined this: "Seek ye first the Kingdom of Heaven"—that is, the highest possible level. That is what a man must really ask for in praying. And since this is the supreme aim of prayer, a man in praying should connect whatever *lesser aim* he asks for with this *supreme aim*, which is the supreme meaning of Man and leads to the highest possible level he can reach.

Chapter Nine

THE SERMON ON THE MOUNT

INTRODUCTION

THE teaching that Christ gives in the Sermon on the Mount lies in between the teaching of John the Baptist and Christ's teaching in parables, about the mysteries of the Kingdom of Heaven. They form three orders of teaching on different levels. The first and most external teaching is that of John the Baptist, of which we find a fragment given in Luke. Then comes in an intermediate position the teaching of the Sermon on the Mount, and finally comes the most internal teaching given in parables about the Kingdom of Heaven. In this chapter we shall take the teaching of John the Baptist as recorded in Luke iii, first, and second, that given in the Sermon on the Mount recorded in Matthew, in conjunction with the Sermon on the Plain recorded in Luke vi.

PART ONE

OF all the strange figures that appear in the Gospels John the Baptist is one of the strangest. Yet perhaps more is said of him *in definition* than is said of any of the others. For example, Christ *defined* him as the highest man of those born of women but added that the least in the Kingdom of Heaven was greater than he. What, then, does John the Baptist represent? What does he stand for in the Gospels? And why is his teaching given first, before Christ comes? Let us look at his teaching, so as to be able to make a comparison between it and that given later on by Christ in the Sermon on the Mount. John taught change of mind (repentance) and the Kingdom of Heaven. He cried: "Repent ye, for the Kingdom of Heaven is at hand." (Matt. iii, 2.) But had he any idea of the nature of the inner change that must take place in a man's mind, and indeed in the whole of him, before the level of the Kingdom is attained? Apparently not, since Christ said he was not of the Kingdom. The

93

fragments of John the Baptist's teaching are given in Luke iii. The multitude are shewn as coming to him for baptism. We must picture him clad in his harsh garment of skin, addressing the people in the following harsh words:

"Ye offspring of vipers, who warned you to flee from the wrath to come? Bring therefore fruits worthy of repentance, and begin not to say within yourselves, We have Abraham to our father: for I say unto you, that God is able of these stones to raise up children unto Abraham."　　　　(Luke iii, 7, 8.)

Notice that the Baptist tells his audience one thing about what change of mind means. He tells them not to say within themselves that they have Abraham "to their father". After he has lashed them all, indiscriminately, in this way, the people naturally ask him what they are supposed to do:

"And the multitudes asked him, saying, What then must we do? And he answered and said unto them, He that hath two coats, let him impart to him that hath none; and he that hath food, let him do likewise. And there came also publicans to be baptized, and they said unto him, Master, what must we do? And he said unto them, Extort no more than that which is appointed you. And soldiers also asked him, saying, And we, what must we do? And he said unto them, Do violence to no man, neither exact anything wrongfully; and be content with your wages."　　　　(Luke iii, 10–14.)

Notice that the question *what to do* is asked three times. And almost as if John the Baptist felt the inadequacy of his answers and his inability to tell them what to do, and his lack of understanding either what the Kingdom meant or what real change of mind in regard to it meant, he goes on to say that another is coming far greater than he:

"And as the people were in expectation, and all men reasoned in their hearts concerning John, whether haply he were the Christ; John answered, saying unto them all, I indeed baptize you with water; but there cometh he that is mightier than I, the latchet of whose shoes I am not worthy to unloose: he shall baptize you with the Holy Ghost and with fire: whose fan is in his hand, throughly to cleanse his threshing-floor, and to gather the wheat into his garner; but the chaff he will burn up with unquenchable fire. With many other exhortations therefore preached he good tidings unto the people."　　　　(Luke iii, 15–18.)

THE SERMON ON THE MOUNT

Now in the Sermon on the Mount, Christ begins by telling his disciples *not what to do* but *what to be* before a man is capable of gaining the Kingdom of Heaven. The Sermon opens with the words: "Blessed are the poor in spirit, for theirs is the Kingdom." Christ is speaking of what a man must *be*, what he must first of all become in himself. A man must become quite different in himself to reach the Kingdom. He must change his mind, change in himself, and become "poor in spirit"—whatever that means. Contrast this with the Baptist's teaching. John is teaching external duties, civilian goodness: Christ is speaking of inner transformation. John thunders at his audience and tells them to repent: Christ speaks of what this inner change, which must come first, means. John tells them *what to do*; Christ *what to be*. Now a man like John the Baptist who was on the external side of the teaching of the Word of God—the teaching about the inner possible evolution of Man—inclines to take everything literally. And the Word of God cannot be taken merely literally, for it is a medium of connexion between the level called "earth" in a man and the possible attainable level called "heaven". Its "earth-meaning" is quite, indeed utterly, different from its "heaven-meaning", and unless its earth-meaning is allowed to grow and develop into new and ever-new meanings, it can make no connexions with the higher level and so is dead. So the literal man, the man who lives in his senses, the man of external meanings alone, who understands nothing internally, and who, if he is religious, follows only the methods and external demands of his sect, cannot develop. Now if John the Baptist was not of the Kingdom, as Christ said distinctly, what does it mean to be *near* the Kingdom? It will help us to understand why the teaching of John the Baptist was not the teaching of the Kingdom. To be near the Kingdom is a question of inner understanding: and there is a clear example of what it means in the Gospels. Let us look at it before going on with the Beatitudes. One of the scribes has asked Jesus what commandment is the first of all. Jesus says: "The Lord is One and thou shalt love the Lord thy God with all thy heart, and with all thy soul, and with all thy understanding, and with all thy strength, and the second is Thou shalt love thy neighbour as thyself." The scribe answers: "Of a truth, Master, thou hast well said, he is One, and there is none other but he, and to love him . . . is much more than whole burnt offerings and sacrifice." "And when Jesus saw that he answered *with his own understanding* (not 'discreetly' as in the translation) he said unto him, Thou art not far from the Kingdom of God. And no man after that durst ask him any question." (Mark xii, 34.) Can we see why the scribe is near the Kingdom? There have always existed those who in religion place much value on external forms and observances and discipline. We read that John the Baptist was puzzled when he heard that Christ and his disciples ate and drank and did not fast literally. And no doubt he would have objected to the disciples plucking the ears of corn on the Sabbath or to Christ's healing on the Sabbath, for it was against the Mosaic Law. At the end of his life the Baptist became (apparently) uncertain about Christ. He even sent a message from prison to Christ saying: "Art thou he that cometh or do we look for another?" (Luke vii, 19.) And what was Christ's reply? Christ replied in such a way that John the Baptist could understand literally. He said: "Go your way, and tell John what things ye have seen and heard; the blind receive their sight, the lame walk, the lepers are cleansed, and the deaf hear, the dead are raised up." John the Baptist could not understand that this meant the *psychologically* deaf, blind, etc. But this *level of understanding* in religion has always existed—the understanding only of the harsh, literal truth, the understanding of the external man, who keeps the teaching of the Word of God on an earth-level and by so doing destroys not only its beauty but its very meaning, as one might destroy a creature with wings by cutting them off. John the Baptist *represents* the literal teaching of the Word of God. He represents the great literal class of such people whom, in the person of the Baptist, Christ defends, since they are the starting-point of all else, and speaks about with such great and obvious care as if they presented a problem very difficult to solve. John the Baptist believed in Christ when he met him, but, as was said, towards the end he is shewn to have doubted. And this is the true *psychological picture* of those who, being grounded in the external side of the teaching of the Word and its harsh literal meaning, meet with the internal or higher meaning of it and are unable to comprehend it and fall back in doubt—and, indeed, feel offended, because they can no longer feel merit, no longer feel themselves better than others. Yet it must be understood that the *literal* meaning of the Word of God must be guarded.

THE first Beatitude, as it is called, is addressed, with the remaining eight, *to Christ's disciples*, and (apparently) not to the multitude. The opening words in the fifth chapter of Matthew are:

> "And seeing the multitudes, he went up into the mountain; and when he had sat down, his disciples came unto him: and he opened his mouth and taught them saying, Blessed are the poor in spirit: for theirs is the kingdom of heaven."
>
> (Matt. v, 1-3.)

In Luke an abbreviated and somewhat different version of the Beatitudes is given, only four being mentioned, and this after Christ has chosen his twelve disciples on the mountain and has descended to the plain. Of these four Beatitudes the first is:

> "Blessed are ye poor: for yours is the kingdom of God."   (Luke vi, 20.)

Since the *poor* only are mentioned in Luke, many have thought that the literally poor are meant. But in Matthew it is said: "Blessed are the *poor in spirit*: for theirs is the kingdom of heaven", and no one can believe that the literally poor are without pride, if one takes the term only in this sense. How then are we really to understand this term "poor in spirit"? In literal translation it is not "poor in spirit" but "beggars in spirit". What does it mean to be a beggar in spirit? Let us clear away all ideas that it means to be literally a beggar or literally poor. There is another word in the Gospels translated as *poor*, which means literally to be poor, as in the case of the story of the widow's mite, where the widow is a woman who is actually poor and gives more than others. But the word used here has a still *lower* meaning. It refers to one who crouches and trembles, as an eastern beggar asking for money at the street-corners, and so has a more powerful psychological meaning. In Luke where, as was said, only four Beatitudes are given, four *woes*, as they are called, are given in a directly opposite correspondence. The corresponding woe to the brief formulation "Blessed are ye poor" is "But woe unto you that are rich, for ye have received your consolation." Now since Matthew says *"poor in spirit"* the meaning of *rich*, in Luke, cannot be anything else but *"rich in spirit"*—that is, it must mean a man who does not *beg* in his spirit, but feels rich in himself and no beggar at all. And he receives his consolation. A man who ascribes everything to himself, who is rich in his own self-complacency and self-esteem, who follows his self-love, his vanity and his sense of being better than others, is *rich in spirit*. A triumph over a rival, a better position, a reward, a clever deal, are his consolations. But if a man feels in his inmost being that he knows nothing and is nothing and deserves nothing, if he longs to understand more and to be different, if he feels that he is really nothing and longs to be something, if in fact in his mind, his spirit, his understanding, he feels his own ignorance, his own nothingness, then he is "poor in spirit". He is empty, and so can be filled. He knows his ignorance and so can *hear* the teaching of the Kingdom. But if he is full of himself, how can he *hear* anything? He hears himself all the time. He hears all the endless voices of his restless complaining vanity, of his satisfied or unsatisfied self-love. When Christ attacked the Pharisees, he was attacking this *richness of spirit*, and of them he said that they had their reward. When he told the rich prince to sell all that he had, he was speaking not of literal possessions, but of that side of a man which makes him believe that by possessions, mental, social and material, he is better than others. And what makes a man especially feel rich in himself is the gratified self-love, the gratified vanity, the merit offered by life. Indeed, the delight of the gratified self-love is stronger than anything else in life and we only have to notice it in ourselves to see that this is true. In this state of equilibrium, due to the self-love, which indeed is so easily upset and makes everyone so easily offended, why should we seek anything else or how should it occur to us that we are nothing and have no real basis in ourselves and actually possess nothing, in view of the higher level of the Kingdom?

Christ continues to speak of what a man *must be*, if he is to draw near the higher level of himself, called the Kingdom:

"Blessed are they that mourn, for they shall be comforted."

The idea that a man can receive inner help or comfort by going against himself is not easy to grasp. Yet if there be a higher level from whence *bliss* proceeds with which communication is possible, the idea is not so remarkable. "Blessed are they that mourn" means that bliss or happiness can reach a person from the higher level of the Kingdom if he *mourns* or if he is *poor in spirit*. But is it to be supposed that a man must go about openly weeping or openly mourning or wearing mourning?

This idea is utterly impossible in view of what Christ teaches in the next chapter of Matthew, the sixth, where it is said that a man must do *everything in secret*—give his alms in *secret*, fast in *secret*, etc., and not do anything for the sake of his self-love, for the sake of praise, and merit, in the eyes of others. Now one mourns the dead in a literal sense. But to feel that one is *dead* in oneself is to mourn in its *psychological* meaning. Christ says many things about the dead—those who are dead, psychologically, internally, in their real inner part that only can evolve to the level of higher Man, but do not know it, and so do not mourn.

The third Beatitude is:

"Blessed are the meek, for they shall inherit the earth."

In the original, the word πρᾶος translated as *meek* is the opposite of the word *angry: resentful*. It has the meaning of becoming *tamed* as a wild animal is tamed. To inherit the earth means here to inherit the land given to the Man of the Kingdom. It is in the same sense as: "Honour thy father and thy mother: that thy days may be long upon the land which the Lord thy God giveth thee." (Exodus xx, 12.) The literal Jews thought the promised land was the land of Canaan. But the inner meaning is the Kingdom of Heaven. The land, then, means the Kingdom, and a man must go against all his natural resentfulness and passion and anger, to become an heir to it.

The fourth Beatitude:

"Blessed are they that hunger and thirst after righteousness for they shall be filled,"

refers to those who long to understand what is that goodness of being and what is that knowledge of Truth that leads to the higher level. They are those who, feeling their nothingness, their ignorance, feeling they are dead in their inner being, long to be taught what Truth the higher Man must know and follow and what Good means at the level of the Kingdom of Heaven. They hunger for Good and thirst for Truth, for the union of these two in a man makes him have the inner harmony called righteousness.

The fifth Beatitude is:

"Blessed are the merciful, for they shall obtain mercy,"

99

one meaning of which is that unless we forgive the sins of others, we cannot expect any mercy ourselves in regard to our own evolution. To have mercy is, in one sense, to know and see that what one blames in others is also in oneself—that is, it is to see the beam in one's own eye, to see *oneself in others* and *others in oneself*. This is one basis of practical mercy. But there are other meanings—as in all things said in the Gospels—one of which is that a man must know about what to have mercy on in himself and about what in himself he must be merciless.

The sixth Beatitude is:

"Blessed are the pure in heart, for they shall see God."

To be pure in heart means literally to be *purged* in heart or cleansed by purgation. It is first about not being a hypocrite. It is about the inner and outer in a man corresponding. It is about an emotional state that can be reached in which the reality of the existence of God is seen directly from the clear-sightedness of the purified emotional understanding, for we understand not only with the mind. The emotional side of a man, when it is filled with self-emotions, and so with bad or evil feeling against those who do not admire him, or with self-pity, with hatred and revenge and so on, is obscured, is in darkness, and cannot fulfil its rightful function of mirroring the higher level. When cleansed, the heart *sees*—that is, understands—the existence of the higher level, of God, of the reality of the teaching of Christ. The purification of the emotions is often dealt with in the Gospels. And let us note that if there were no higher level, there could be no purification of the emotions beyond the self-emotions.

The seventh Beatitude is:

"Blessed are the peace-makers for they shall be called the sons of God."

To make peace in oneself is to be free from inner disharmonies, inner disturbances, inner contradictions. To make peace with others is to act always from what is Good and not to take hold of differences of opinion or argue about different view-points or theories, which always produce disagreements. If people acted from Good and not from divergence in theories and viewpoints—that is, from their different ideas of Truth, they would be peacemakers. They are here called "Sons of God" because here God is taken as *Good* itself—in exactly the sense in which Christ defined God, when someone called Christ "Good Master", and Christ said to him:

"Why callest thou me good? None is good save one, even God" (Luke xviii, 19). Hatred divides all: Good unites all and so is *One*, and that is God.

Now follow two further Beatitudes which, in this brief consideration, can be taken together, as they both refer to what it means to act *beyond the self-love* and all the merit connected with it:

> "Blessed are they that have been persecuted for righteousness' sake: for theirs is the kingdom of heaven. Blessed are ye when men shall reproach you, and persecute you, and say all manner of evil against you falsely, for my sake. Rejoice, and be exceeding glad: for great is your reward in heaven."
>
> (Matt. v, 10–12.)

In Luke this idea is expressed thus:

> "Blessed are ye when men shall hate you, and when they shall separate you from their company, and reproach you, and cast out your name as evil, for the Son of man's sake. Rejoice in that day, and leap for joy: for behold your reward is great in heaven:"

and the corresponding *woe* is rendered thus: "woe unto you when all men shall speak well of you!" (Luke vi, 22, 23, 26.)

Here, and in every one of the Beatitudes, Christ is speaking of a man who after long inner psychological work on himself begins to *desire* what is beyond his self-love. He is speaking of a man who is no longer centred in his self-love, but seeks to escape from it. And it is just here that the most difficult psychological barrier lies. But even to catch a glimpse of it, though we are unable to cross it, is of incalculable value. For who, leading a good and respectable life, and acting from, let us say, the level of the teaching of John the Baptist, will be able to escape the feeling of merit and will in any sense be able to rejoice when men speak evil of him? A man, a good man in life—and this is what John the Baptist taught about and so he is the starting-point of all else—may very well feel that he does his best to behave rightly, that he gives away his spare clothing, that he gives food to those who have none, that he extorts no more than is legally due to him, that he does no violence, exacts nothing wrongfully, and that he is content with his pay. But how will he escape the final *merit* of all this? For wherever the self-love is involved, and however good a person is from the level of self-love, which is the first level of everyone, there lies a great psychological problem about which Christ spoke in endless ways and about which so many whom he addressed felt the greatest offence. The self-love, which ascribes all to itself, cannot reach the level of the Kingdom, and in the Beatitudes we can see what a man must first become, what he must first *be* in himself, as distinct from the man of self-love and merit and virtue, before the Kingdom comes within sight.

There follows now the summing up of the whole meaning of the Beatitudes in the strange terms of *salt* and *having salt* and of the *salt losing its savour*. Christ continues as follows. (He is still speaking to his disciples.)

"Ye are the salt of the earth, but if the salt have lost its savour (literally, 'become foolish') wherewith shall it be salted? it is thenceforth good for nothing, but to be cast out and trodden under foot of men."   (Matt. v, 13.)

Salt is, technically in this case (as well as actually), a conjunction of two things, of two distinct elements. It represents a union. We have already seen elsewhere that all knowledge of Truth, all Truth itself, leads as its goal to its own Good and its own use. Every Truth seeks union with its own Good. Truth by itself is useless. And Good without Truth is again useless . . . The Beatitudes are about reaching a certain inner state of *desire* that can lead to union, for all desire seeks union as its fulfilment. The Truth of the teaching of Christ, or the knowledge of the Word of God, or the Truth about Man's inner evolution, is nothing if practised by itself, without any realisation of its goal, which is the Good it leads to: and the union of the two is bliss—not the ordinary happiness we know in life which so soon can turn into its opposite—but a state that is complete and full in itself and so self-creating through its own power because it has the two elements Truth and Good in union. This is the *marriage feast* in the Gospels—the marriage of the two things in a man which constitute the whole of his inner life. This is the turning of the water of Truth into wine, at the marriage feast at Cana of Galilee. For a man, seen internally, apart from his outer body and semblance, is first his knowledge of Truth and his level of Good: and finally, in his evolution, he becomes the marriage of these two. He then has (in one sense only) what in the Gospels is called "life in himself" because from this union he receives power from a higher level. It is perhaps possible to understand that a man may practise the side of Truth without having any desire for it to lead anywhere save into the self-esteem. Then he has no desire for the

Truth he follows to lead to its awaiting Good. He has no desire for this union, for this inner mystery of the conjunction. He does not want what he *knows* to transform what he *is* and ultimately to unite with its own goal by finding the Good in him that belongs to it. Then he has no *salt*. He is acting without the right desire. He is making the salt *foolish*. And having no real understanding of what he is doing, he will easily confuse what teaching he knows with his ordinary life and with all the reactions of his ordinary life. Not seeing where the Truth leads, or what is its goal, he will take it on his own level, as an end in itself, and even make it a fresh source of feeling dislike, rivalry, jealousy and superiority over others, and even of cruelty. He will be blind to the Good of the teaching he has received as the real goal. This is why Christ said, in another place, after his disciples had been quarrelling with one another as to who was the greatest:

"Salt is good, but if the salt have lost its savour wherewith will ye season it? *Have salt in yourselves*: and *be at peace* one with another."   (Mark ix, 50.)

The disciples are quarrelling from their self-love and have forgotten their aim. And it is just because people forget why they are trying to follow the teaching of Truth and do not really wish to be different and realise another goodness, and so mix everything up, both old and new, that Christ says: "Seek ye *first* the Kingdom of Heaven and its righteousness and all else shall be added unto you."

Chapter Ten

FAITH

PART ONE

WHAT is faith? People may imagine that they know what faith means. But *faith* is not easy to understand. It is called in the Gospels a seed, in a man's mind. Christ says: "If ye have faith as a grain of mustard *seed*, ye shall say unto this mountain, Remove hence to yonder place, and it shall remove." And he adds these strange words: "and nothing shall be impossible unto you." Christ spoke these words to his disciples when they had failed to cure the epileptic boy and had asked why they were unable to do so. The first answer to their question is: "Because of your little faith." The event is related as follows:

"There came to him a man kneeling to him, and saying, Lord, have mercy on my son: for he is epileptic, and suffereth grievously: for oft-times he falleth into the fire, and oft-times into the water. And I brought him to thy disciples, and they could not cure him. And Jesus answered and said, O faithless and perverse generation, how long shall I be with you? how long shall I bear with you? bring him hither to me. And Jesus rebuked him; and the devil went out from him: and the boy was cured from that hour. Then came the disciples to Jesus apart, and said, Why could not we cast it out? And he saith unto them, Because of your little faith: for verily I say unto you, If ye have faith as a grain of mustard seed, ye shall say unto this mountain, Remove hence to yonder place; and it shall remove; and nothing shall be impossible unto you."

(Matt. xvii, 14–21.)

The disciples are told they failed because they had "little faith", but in some ancient versions of the Gospels Christ is said to have replied that they failed because they had *no faith*, and many commentators say that the words "little faith" were probably substituted as an interpretation of the original drastic words: "because ye have no faith."

Among many other divisions, in the Gospels, men are divided into those *who have faith* and those *who have no faith*. But it seems strange that the disciples who believed in Christ, who, in fact, are said to have given up everything in order to follow him, are told that they belong to those who have no faith. Let us try to understand what is meant. Faith is not, as people suppose, *belief*. Nicodemus believed in Christ because he wrought miracles, but Christ brushed this aside, and said to him: "Except a man be born anew, he cannot see the Kingdom of God." Faith is something more than mere belief. Christ defines it as a *seed* and a seed is something that is organised and has its own life in itself, and can grow by itself. If a man has a seed of faith in him that man is alive exactly in the sense in which it is said in the Parable of the Prodigal Son: "For this my son was dead and is alive again." You will remember that in this parable it is said that the younger son "came to himself" and, turning round, began to "return to his father"—that is, to go in one direction. Let us consider first of all this idea of going in one direction, in connexion with the meaning of faith, and at the same time let us understand that it is not easy to grasp what *faith* means. In the incident quoted above, when Christ was told that the disciples could not cure the epileptic boy he at once exclaimed: "O faithless and *perverse* generation!" It is of the greatest importance to understand these words, because they throw the first light on the meaning of faith. What does this word *perverse* mean and why does it follow immediately after the word *faithless*? At first sight there seems to be no connexion between these two adjectives. This generation is called faithless and *perverse*. What is the connexion? In the Greek the meaning of the word translated as "perverse" signifies "turning in many directions". This means that to have *no faith*, to be entirely lacking in the quality of faith—hence to be "faithless"—is linked with turning in many different directions and so to have no one direction to follow. What Christ says is: "O generation without faith and turning in all directions." A man without faith, a faithless man, is *perverse* in this sense. He turns in many different directions, not ever knowing where he is going. And in ordinary life people all the time are turning in different directions, at one moment believing in one thing or in one mood, and the next moment in another thing or in another mood. It is only necessary to observe *oneself* to see the truth of this. Is it not true to say that one is turned in a different direction by nearly every book that one reads, every opinion that one hears, by every change of circumstance and fashion? And does not every mood paint life in different colours? But people imagine that they have permanent inner stability and it is true that as long as the general conditions of life remain the same they feel a kind of stability, but it is rarely due to anything in themselves. We have only to read history to see how aimless life is, in the deepest sense.

The incident of the epileptic boy and the failure of the disciples to cure him owing to their having no faith is related immediately after the account of the Transfiguration of Christ:

"And after six days, Jesus taketh with him Peter, and James, and John his brother, and bringeth them up into a high mountain apart: and he was transfigured before them; and his face did shine as the sun, and his garments became white as the light." (Matt. xvii, 1, 2.)

And after they had come down from the Mount of Transfiguration what did they meet? They met the dark evil insane world below typified by the epileptic boy casting himself now into fire and now into water, surrounded by the multitude without faith and turning in all directions. This is the contrast that is drawn. Mankind, without faith, is like the epileptic boy—the boy described actually as being *under the power of the moon*, for, in the Greek, the word translated as epileptic means literally "moon-struck" and so "lunatic" or "insane". And we can see, in this connexion of narrated events and Christ's words when he comes down from the Mount of Transfiguration to the level of life, a significant bearing on the meaning of *faith*. When it is said that Christ went up the mount, into a high mountain, apart, and was transfigured—and literally, in the Greek, this means *metamorphosis* or transformation of form, a going beyond all ordinary form, just as μετάνοια means a going beyond one's ordinary mind, one's ordinary forms of thought— the meaning is that a higher form of Man exists as a possibility and that faith is something that belongs to this idea about Man—to the idea of the possible transformation of Man. Christ was transformed before his three disciples. He shewed them, in some way impossible to understand and merely described in terms of ascending a high mountain, that the transformation of Man is a reality. He proved it to them in some way—how, we do not know. But they could scarcely comprehend it and not only were afraid but, as it says in one account, were so *asleep* that they could take in nothing of what was happening until they were brought into a full *waking state*. In Luke this is put clearly enough in the following words: "Now Peter and they that were with him were weighed down with sleep: but when they were fully awake they saw his glory . . ." (Luke ix, 32.) And it would be a great mistake to think that merely physical sleep is meant here. It was the day-time. Why should the disciples be heavy with sleep in the day-time? Even if they were, why mention such a detail? The *sleep* that is meant here is not ordinary sleep. In the Gospels many words which have an ordinary meaning are used in a special way and have a quite different meaning. For example, the word "dead" when used in the Gospels does not necessarily refer to physical death. *Dead people*, from the point of view of the teaching about Man in the Gospels, are not people in the grave but people walking about. When Christ says: "Let the dead bury their dead," (Matt. viii, 22) obviously he is not referring to people who are literally dead. How can literally dead people bury literally dead people? Men are divided into the *dead* and the *living* with a special significance. The phrase "the quick and the dead" refers to people who have something alive in themselves, and to those who have not and so are dead already. A man immersed in life who can see nothing save the interests of the world, of power, of money, and position and rivalry, is *dead*. In the same way men are divided into those who are *asleep* and those *awake*. The man who is beginning to awaken is a man who is not merely capable of comprehending meaning beyond the meanings of ordinary life but is certain of its reality: and to comprehend and to be certain that there is meaning beyond life and that earthly life does not explain Man is to begin to *awaken from sleep*. The disciples were not literally asleep in the ordinary sense but they were literally asleep in another sense. They were asleep to greater meaning. They were mentally and emotionally asleep to the idea of the ultimate meaning of human life that Christ revealed to them by his transfiguration. They were asleep to the whole idea of the transformation of Man, for they are represented in many passages as merely believing that Christ was the destined Messiah, the deliverer of an oppressed nation, and that he was going to found a magnificent kingdom on earth in which they would occupy the highest positions and have the largest possessions and the greatest power. And so, blind to Christ's teaching about the Kingdom of Heaven, and asleep to this idea of the transformation of Man, when in the presence of the actual manifestation before them, they were said to be weighed down with sleep. The quality of their minds, their degree of *consciousness*, their level of understanding, could not reach to it. No man can realise anything, or perceive the existence of anything, that demands a higher mental and conscious state. A man is asleep to what he does not understand. For to the vast majority of people, whatever they are ignorant of does not exist for them and they ridicule its possible existence. These are among the ordinary limiting factors that confine Mankind to its state. But there are special factors that limit even the most educated part of Mankind, due to their quality of understanding and the degree of their consciousness.

Faith is connected with the idea of *transformation* and so is not mere belief, on the ordinary plane, as when a person might believe in this man or not believe in him, as the case may be. As we shall see later, in another narrative bearing on the real meaning of *faith*—when the conversation of the centurion with Christ is mentioned—*faith*, in its essential meaning, denotes a conviction, a certainty, that a higher interpretation of life exists, and as a consequence, that the transformation of Man is a possibility. The peculiar quality of *faith* lies in this idea, that life can only be understood and solved by the sense of something higher than Man as he is, and that Man has this possibility of becoming transformed and passing into entirely new meanings in regard to his life on earth. It is this peculiar quality that is the essence of *faith* and renders it utterly different from what we usually call belief. Faith, in fact, undermines all our ordinary and natural beliefs because it leads *away* from worldly belief and in a direction that can no longer be confirmed by natural belief and the evidence of sense. And for this reason it is defined as a *seed* in a man's mind—that is, it is the potentiality of a growth in a man's mind which cannot exist in him as long as he believes that life, as it is, is the end of Man, and not a means to something else. For if we imagine life is an end in itself and the only end, we cannot possess faith and do not wish it. But if the thought enters our minds that life cannot be an end in itself, but must be a means to another end—and often such thoughts occur to everyone—then, precisely in this moment of *new thinking*, there is the foreshadowing of *faith*. Christ in the moment of transformation represents men at a higher level of himself—a far higher level. His descent from the mount represents the coming down to the plane of ordinary earthly life—a level of madness, insanity, a level governed as it were by the waxing and waning moon. And all these ideas are dramatised in the scene of the Mount of Transfiguration and far below was the epileptic boy whom the disciples could not cure.

PART TWO

Iᴛ has been already seen that *faith* is compared with a living active *seed* in a man
and is not merely passive belief. In order to understand something further about
the meaning of faith, let us look at what is said about the *result* of possessing faith.
Christ says: "If ye have faith as a grain of mustard seed . . . nothing shall be impossible unto you." The result of having faith is that nothing is impossible to a
man. The possession of faith renders what was impossible possible. In another place
—in the corresponding account given in the ninth chapter of Mark—the phrase is
"All things are possible to him who has faith." At first sight, it might be thought
that this means that a man having faith has the *power to do*. But this is not quite what
is said. The possession of faith renders things *possible*, and this is a different idea.
To a man who has faith things become possible that otherwise are impossible.
It is not the man himself but the faith in him that renders things possible. To a man
of faith all things become possible and nothing is impossible. Our ordinary idea
of power is more or less connected with violence. For instance, people can be
forced to obey. But the idea of the power that is given by faith is different. In the
presence of a man who really possesses faith, in Christ's sense, things become
possible. Such a man has power because, through his possessing faith, all things
no longer have their own power and so become possible to him. Things are robbed
of their ordinary natural power and especially of harmful power, and this idea is
often met with in the New Testament and in one place is expressed in the following words: "And these signs shall follow them that have faith . . . they shall take up
serpents, and if they drink any deadly thing it shall in no wise hurt them and they
shall lay hands on the sick and they shall recover" (Mark xvi, 17–18). The robbing
of the ordinary power of things, by means of faith, is shewn in the above verse.
In this respect faith is like Truth. Truth has no power over lies, save by rendering
lies powerless. For example, if a man allows the Truth to enter his mind in the
midst of all his lying, the lies lose all power over him and for the moment he
becomes sane.

The disciples had done their best and could not cure the epileptic boy. They
had used their own powers, but, as the father tells Christ in the account in Mark:
"they had no force" (Mark ix, 18). And Christ at once exclaims: "O generation
without faith, how long shall I endure you?" The disciples ask him privately why

they failed. The reply is: "Because you have no faith." The thing was impossible to them because they did not possess the smallest *seed of faith*. Yet they were the disciples of Christ. Nor would they have *faith* after seeing the epileptic boy cured, for faith does not come from externally-seen miracles and passive belief in them. Because they had no faith, the cure of the boy was impossible for them. The situation would not surrender to them. The necessary factor to make the situation yield up its own power was lacking in them. The father of the boy says to Christ: "If thou hast the power, help us." Christ exclaims: "If thou hast the power! All things are possible to him who has faith." The father, despairing, cries: "I have faith—help my absence of faith." Both in Mark and in Matthew the accounts of the cure are used to bring a strong light to bear on the idea of faith and the power that results from its possession. Faith—πίστις—is connected with a certain power —δύναμις—that is, faith is dynamic in a special way. But the power of faith is not gained from outside, from position, from worldly power, or from anything external. Nor is faith the evidence of things seen; it does not derive its power from that source. It is not formed in that external part of the mind that deals with life and things, or with all the duties and cares of human existence. It is not *on this level*. It belongs to a level of mind above ordinary visible things. It is like a point offered to a man that lies *above himself*. It is, as it were, as if he were to open a communication with a room of the floor above the room he usually dwells in, where people live another kind of life and of which his own strength of conviction has led him to feel the existence, and discover it for himself. For the idea of faith cannot be understood unless the idea of different levels in Man is understood. Man does not live at the highest level of himself. A level awaits him. He is not complete. And he only can complete himself. Nothing *external* can complete him—that is, can bring him to his highest development. Unless he is convinced that this is his real explanation, his mind remains shut to this possibility—that is, to anything higher. What is higher is *in him*; but it is as yet unknown, unvisited. A new meaning arises in him when he feels the conviction of this idea. A new birth is possible. Another level of thought and feeling and understanding is possible. A New *Man* is hidden in every man. For this reason the Gospels do not speak of life, or of how to get on in life, but about this New *Man* concealed in every man. Their teaching is about a higher level—that is, about *the evolution of a man*. The idea that a man can be different is not confined to the teaching in the Gospels.

It is found in many ancient teachings. It is the only real basis of any *psychology of Man*. The real psychology of an acorn must be based on the fact that it can become an oak-tree; otherwise its existence can only be accounted for wrongly and quite wrong views invented about it. In the structure of the nervous system we find many definite and quite distinct *levels*, one above the other, where things are arranged and represented in quite different ways. A lower level cannot understand a higher one and a lower level must obey a higher because it surrenders its power to it. A man has only to think of moving his arm and he can do so. All the lower levels obey the thought. So a man, working through the evidence of his senses and thinking at that mental level, cannot understand *faith*. Faith is already the absolute certainty of a higher level and so already it opens the influence of a higher level to act in a man. Let us look, in this connexion, at another parable about the meaning of faith, expressed by means of the incident of the centurion:

"And a certain centurion's servant, who was dear unto him, was sick, and at the point of death. And when he heard concerning Jesus, he sent unto him elders of the Jews, asking him that he would come and save his servant. And they, when they came to Jesus, besought him earnestly, saying, He is worthy that thou shouldest do this for him: for he loveth our nation, and himself built us our synagogue. And Jesus went with them. And when he was now not far from the house, the centurion sent friends to him, saying unto him, Lord, trouble not thyself: for I am not worthy that thou shouldest come under my roof: wherefore neither thought I myself worthy to come unto thee: but say the word and my servant shall be healed. For I also am a man set under authority, having under myself soldiers: and I say unto this one, Go, and he goeth; and to another, Come, and he cometh, and to my servant, Do this, and he doeth it. And when Jesus heard these things, he marvelled at him, and turned and said unto the multitude that followed him, I say unto you, I have not found so great faith, no, not in Israel. And they that were sent, returning to the house, found the servant whole."   (Luke vii, 2–10.)

Why should Christ say here that he has never met with greater faith? The centurion expressed in his words the essential idea of faith. He knows from his experiences as a soldier that there is a higher and a lower—that is, what is above and what is below him- and from this, as a result of his own thought, he is convinced that a higher and a lower exist, not only in the external visible world. The centurion says: "Neither thought I myself worthy to come to thee." Here the word *worthy* means in the Greek on the same *level*. The centurion understood *levels* of Man. He understood that everything is a question of *levels*—that is he understood *higher and lower as a principle* and knew that a lower level must obey a higher level, in the very nature of things. He knew first of all that Christ was on a higher level than himself. He realised that all that Christ did and said was from a *higher level* than the level that he, the centurion, acted and spoke from. In the second place he knew that Christ also *obeyed a higher level* just as he, the centurion, obeyed those over him, who had greater authority than he possessed. And in how many places in the Gospels does not Christ indicate in the clearest way this obedience to what is higher? He was not free. He was obeying another will and through this had power. What power could the centurion possess if he did not obey those over him? By obedience to those above him he had power over those below him. None of his soldiers below him would have obeyed him unless he himself obeyed those above him. He understood this and so discerned the source of Christ's power, so that Christ exclaims: "I say unto you, I have not found so great faith, no, not in Israel."

Since the idea of faith is connected with the power of making things obey, it is clearly also connected with the power that a man may gain over himself, in the sense of making all that is in him, all his different desires, different momentary wills, different thoughts, moods, etc., obey something in him owing to the fact that this something in him is of such a nature that it deprives all these different things of any power to affect him. The Greek word for faith—πίστις—is from the verb πειθω, which means to persuade, or *make to obey*. What in a man will make all sides of himself obey him? What persuasion in his mind will bring him into a position where everything in him will yield its power to him? If a man could find this secret he would be master of himself, not directly, through his own power, but through the power given him by faith.

It is just here that a man must *create himself*. And this task of self-creation cannot be haphazard. It must be based on ideas that transcend ordinary meanings. To believe in what we can see does not create us. Out of all we witness we may pick out this or that aspect and hold to it as Truth. But such Truth is external and its source is from visible life. The source of faith is from invisible life. The disciples had no *faith* because they were merely impressed by Christ as an extra-ordinary man and by the miracles. And in a sense, as long as Christ was among them, a visible body, they could not have *faith* and so could not *create themselves*. In a sense Christ tested them by being rough with them. Christ offended people right and left. Even his disciples, like many others who listened to his teaching, were *afraid to ask questions*. It is said in Matthew that after Christ had confounded the Pharisees (who had said that the Christ was the son of David) by the words: "If David then calleth him Lord, how is he his son?" no one was able to answer him, "neither durst any man from that day forth ask him any more questions." And we read in Mark that even the disciples, when Christ was teaching them about his coming death and resurrection, "understood not the saying, and were afraid to ask him." The object was to make them believe not *because of*, but *in spite of* all that took place—and the crucifixion, the most dishonourable of all forms of death, was in itself a test apart from its other meanings. Then after they were left only with what they had been taught—with certain strange ideas, parables, sayings, and perhaps with very much of which no record was ever attempted, they had to turn all they had seen and heard—all that had been taken in by the channel of the senses, into this *living seed* called faith. They had to be deprived of its outer basis, before it could be established in them on a new basis according to the promise that Christ had made to them: "The Comforter, even the Holy Spirit, whom the Father will send in my name, he shall teach you all things, and bring to your remembrance all that I said to you" (John xiv, 26).

People either argue that God does not exist because horrible things happen on earth, or they say: if anything higher exists, why are we not told exactly what it is, and what we have to do and so on? To the first argument the answer has been given: it is expressly said that God's will is not done on earth. To the second, the answer is that people cannot evolve—that is, come into a new birth of them-selves—by mere external example or indeed by any form of thought or idea based on the senses. Truth that can work in a man towards self-change can be sown into him by this channel and must be. But by itself, falling on all that is sense-based in his mind, it falls "by the wayside" and is destroyed. A man must hear and receive *beyond himself*—beyond anything that he has acquired from contact with ordinary life and its problems and proofs, beyond all ordinary notions and his limited powers of comprehending, which he has got from time and space. Everything that can renew, regenerate and change him must be raised up beyond *that level*, simply because its true function is to open up in him *another level*. So it is germinal, and though coming from outside is of a higher destiny, in belonging to a higher degree of a man: and is, in short, the first of a series of connecting ideas and thoughts, the first ferment or leaven, that leads to a communication with that higher level, and a transformation in understanding the meaning of a man's life on earth. For if we think of the evolution of a man as the inner connecting up with an already existing possibility—just as an oak-tree is a *possibility* in an acorn, being a *higher level* of an acorn—and that this connecting up can only be possible through a growing intensity of insight and conviction which enables a man to tilt the balance in himself, as it were, and point in a new direction—in this *one* and single direction that Christ is so constantly speaking of in metaphor and parable—then we can more easily understand that passive belief through what the senses prove is useless and that faith must be something alive and constantly at work in a man to effect its supreme art, its *alchemy*—which is the creation of a New Man in a man. And in this process the laws of another order higher than his own must begin to influence and affect a man, just as, for an acorn to undergo its latent possible transformation, it must begin to obey the laws of oak-trees and gradually cease being an acorn at all.

PART THREE

THE disciples said to Christ: "Increase our faith." What answer did they receive and what light does it throw on the meaning of the word *faith* used so technically in the Gospels, and so difficult to understand, and which people think means belief?

The occasion on which the disciples asked this question is given in the seventeenth chapter of Luke. Christ is represented as first speaking of the difficulties of *living* the teaching. Difficulties were bound to arise. Simply to begin to try to practise the teaching did not at once do away with all troubles. Christ says to them: "It is impossible but that occasions of stumbling shall come. But woe unto him through whom they come." He is speaking of the difficulties that must arise among those who followed the teaching. And even then they probably could not understand they were being taught an inner discipline. He continues: "It were well for him if a millstone were hanged about his neck and he were thrown into the sea, rather than that he should cause one of these little ones to stumble." This refers not to little children, but to those who are just trying to understand the teaching of Christ. They are little in understanding (in the Greek μικρός—microscopical—which has nothing to do with little children). The disciples had to learn that they had to teach others. As long as they thought that in following Christ they were following a future king on earth this must have been a strange idea. Christ is then represented as saying: "Take heed to yourselves"—(literally, pay attention to yourselves)—"If thy brother sin, rebuke him: and if he repent, forgive him. And if he sin against thee seven times in the day and seven times turn to thee, saying I repent: thou shalt forgive him."

Christ is speaking of how a man must *behave* in the teaching. People take knowledge apart from behaviour. He must *behave* in a certain way to others in the teaching. The disciples may have perceived that in order to behave in this way, it was necessary to have *faith* or else it would be impossible. Taken quite literally, to forgive a man seven times a day is not easy, even if he repents.

The disciples then make their request. "And the apostles said unto the Lord, Increase our faith." (Literally, they say: "Add to our faith.") The way in which faith can be added to or increased is not immediately mentioned. Christ replies by saying *"if ye had faith"*—implying here as elsewhere that they had not. "If ye had faith as a grain of mustard seed, ye would say unto this sycamine tree; Be thou rooted up, and be thou planted in the sea; and it would have obeyed you." Every obstacle, every natural difficulty, is rendered powerless and must obey the will of a man who possesses faith—not his ordinary will but the will arising from another level and source in him opened by faith. Christ then describes how faith is increased, in words that do not seem directly connected with the disciples' demand and which are not always taken as being the answer. He says:

"But which of you, having a servant plowing or keeping sheep, will say unto him by and by, when he is come from the field, Go and sit down to meat? And will not rather say unto him, Make ready wherewith I may sup, and gird thyself and serve me, till I have eaten and drunken; and afterward thou shalt eat and drink? Doth he thank the servant because he did the things that were commanded him? I trow not. So likewise ye, when ye shall have done all those things which are commanded you, say, We are unprofitable servants: we have done that which it was our duty to do."

(Luke xvii, 7–10.)

What is the meaning lying behind this ordinary illustration? How does it contain the answer to the disciples' request: "Add faith to us."

A certain attitude is necessary for faith to exist and increase. What is the nature of this attitude? A man must realise he is *under authority*. The centurion realised this, and, in realising it, understood one thing. He knew what faith depended on and so in a way what faith is.

Faith is the convinced and certain realisation of a *higher level* to which a man must subject everything in him. He cannot do as he pleases. But in life everyone feels he can and should do as he pleases. He must bring himself to obey this higher level that lies in himself. A man possessing faith is no longer one man—just the "man in life"—but two men. A separation has begun to take place in him, dividing him into two. He is a "man in life" and a man aware of "another life": not another life after death, but another life *now*, possible to him *now*. There is an external "life" side which looks to outer life, to the world as seen, and all its rewards: and an internal side which looks to this higher level of whose existence he has become finally convinced and which he knows and feels lies *within him*.

When a man is thus *two*, his attitude to himself and to life entirely changes. He is aware of a higher and a lower level in himself.

Formerly all he did, however good, was done from the lower level in him and remained there. And when this is the case a man cannot help looking for *merit* and reward in all he does, and ascribing to himself his own goodness or greatness or longsuffering. He cannot help doing so. Nor can he help expecting a reward for everything extra, everything additional that he does, for every act of usefulness, every praiseworthy deed, every extra effort. His Good is in the world —that is, the reigning principle of the level of evolution he is at. He does everything *in a certain way*. Everything is tainted with *himself*, with *meritoriousness*, with *goodness*, with the idea of a *reward*. This is his level of *being*, the level he lives at, the only level he knows. Because he has no *faith*, he has no idea of a higher level. He has no idea of *a higher level of himself* to which he seeks to be united.

His being, *himself*, his *self-liking*, will absorb everything. In consequence he will secretly hate people who disagree with him or who do not praise him or laugh at him, although he may not shew it outwardly in case his reputation would suffer. He will find no remedy for this, because he takes himself *as he is*; and so cannot change. He merely wants to be *better*, not different. He wants to be the *same* man, but better—not another man, a man *reborn*.

All that Christ taught was about attaining a higher level, called *re-birth*. His teaching was about *evolution*—about the evolution possible and *awaiting Man*.

It was not a teaching merely about remaining the *same* man and becoming a slightly better man, but about becoming a New Man born of "water and spirit" —that is, of faith and its truth—and living according to the spirit of it—i.e. *willing* it. For if another level exists in every man, the attainment of it can only be through studying the *knowledge* reaching Man from it and living it. All the sayings and parables in the Gospels are *knowledge* about this higher level, this higher possible *degree of Man*. This is their explanation. This *knowledge* is not like knowledge gained through visible life and the senses which is easily verified. It must be understood by the *mind*. This is *faith*.

Faith is not believing in the *extraordinary* because miracles are performed but a perception, an insight, and a conviction that there is an order of Truth above the truth of the senses: and one that the senses cannot give directly—that is, they cannot form the starting-point. A man must start *beyond himself*—and *faith* is the starting-point. And here all he has thought and silently understood in the solitariness of his own mind counts. All that he cannot speak of, all that is most *internal* in him and so beyond the external sense-driven side of him—which is actually the machine in him—counts. For all such thoughts belong to something that can take hold of knowledge—that is, faith—and make a connexion with the *higher* or more *interior* level, the reaching of which is the true evolution of him and the meaning of his complex existence. These private thoughts, speculations, weavings, fantasies, imaginings, ponderings, all apparently aimless and reaching back to childhood and innocence, belong to a man's *deepest and most significant side*. But they are so, only because they can form a starting-point for the knowledge of *faith*. For even if a man meets with real knowledge, as did the disciples of Christ, what is taught him via the external sense-hearing side can only *combine* with him if it is pondered, privately thought of and speculated upon, imagined and finally grasped *by this inner deeper side of him*. Christ did not expect the disciples to *understand* what he said. He knew they could not as yet. People imagine they can understand if merely told. But people have been *told* things from the beginning of time. And many know quite well that if they think externally of themselves and of what they are like, nothing happens. To think of oneself in such a way as to begin *to change oneself* in the light of new ideas, new knowledge, new Truth and new understanding is not something anyone can just do. Yet people address one another and find fault with one another as if they could change at once. Nay, it is not too much to say that none can change, neither by his own circle of ideas nor by new knowledge—unless an inner consent due to an inner and strange realisation in the very heart precedes his attempt and forms the entry into another understanding. For no one can be changed by outer things or by his outer thoughts. Nor can anyone be changed by compulsion. Nothing done in the world in the way of new arrangements, adjustments, social systems and regulations and so on, can change a man *in himself*. Only he, awaking to Truth and seeing Truth in the light of Truth and no longer in the light of self-interest and expediency, can begin to change. For he can only change *from what he has seen for himself* and never from what he is told.

*   *   *

What then is the meaning of the parable that refers to faith? A man must be willing to act *beyond himself* to increase faith. What he does is nothing. To obey the knowledge that is of *faith*, he must act in life differently from other people. How does an ordinary man act in life? He reckons up what is due to him. If he feels he is doing more than others he complains. All life is like that and all men are like that. Everyone is jealous of everyone else. Everyone thinks he is unfairly treated, or that he should have a better reward. *That is human life.* For a man to behave differently, he must have another *feeling of life* and another *feeling of himself*. In the light of a new understanding all that he does, and all efforts that he makes, must appear to him to be nothing. No credit and debit account can be made. The Parable of the Unprofitable Servant, however, is not merely about life. It is about life in the circle of teaching, in the *school*, that Christ was establishing. In that teaching of that school, everything that a man had to do—was nothing. He must not feel any merit for it. It was nothing but his duty. To feel merit would destroy *faith*. It would mean that he felt only the ordinary level of himself with its ordinary meanings. With such standards no one could work, no one could change, no one could become different. For if a man always feels in the same way and has the same ideas and the same limits within him, how can he change? He must go *beyond himself* to become different. And if he does so, he must regard it as *nothing*. Feeling in the knowledge that is faith, and in the conviction of something above himself, his own poverty and ignorance, whatever the efforts he makes he sees as *nothing*. He takes no reward, no meritoriousness. He knows he is an unprofitable, a useless servant.

PART FOUR

THERE are some parables about faith where some action is described and its bearing on the meaning of faith is not immediately clear. As an example, take the parable of the woman who was a sinner, as related in Luke:

"And behold, a woman in the city who was a sinner, when she knew that he sat at meat in the Pharisee's house, brought an alabaster box of ointment, and stood at his feet behind him weeping, and began to wet his feet with her tears, and wiped them with the hair of her head, and kissed his feet, and anointed them with the ointment. Now when the Pharisee who had bidden him saw it, he spake within himself, saying: This man if he were a prophet would know who and what manner of woman this is that toucheth him; for she is a sinner. And Jesus answering said unto him: Simon, I have somewhat to say unto thee. And he saith: Master, say on. A certain creditor had two debtors; the one owed five hundred pence, and the other fifty; and when they had nothing to pay, he freely forgave them both. Tell me therefore, which of them will love him most? Simon answered and said: He I suppose to whom he forgave the most. And he said unto him: Thou hast rightly judged. And he turned to the woman, and said unto Simon: Seest thou this woman? I entered into thy house, thou gavest me no water for my feet; but she hath wet my feet with her tears, and wiped them with her hair. Thou gavest me no kiss; but she since the time I came in hath not ceased to kiss my feet. My head with oil thou didst not anoint; but she hath anointed my feet with ointment. Wherefore I say unto thee, Her many sins are forgiven; for she loved much; but to whom little is forgiven, the same loveth little. And he said unto her: Thy sins are forgiven. And they that sat at meat with him began to say within themselves; Who is this that forgiveth sins also? And he said to the woman: Thy faith hath saved thee; go in peace." (Luke vii, 37-50.)

In the parable Simon is drawn as a certain kind of man, who loves little. The consequence is shewn: because he loves little he can be forgiven little. The woman who was a sinner is contrasted with him. Because she loves much, she can be forgiven much. But the connexion with the meaning of faith is not yet clear.

Simon was a Pharisee—that is, he represented that kind of man who practises religion as a means of ostentation, of appearance and so of increasing self-merit. Such a man does everything for self-love, not for "love of God or neighbour". And everything done for self-love can only go into self and so increase the feeling of meritoriousness.

Self-love is not love. The Pharisee is continually held up throughout the Gospels as the example of all those whose actions are based on self-love, on attracting attention, on reputation, and who therefore can do nothing, however charitable it seems, without the feeling of merit. And if a man does everything from merit, he cannot help thinking himself better than others and expecting a reward for what he does. The woman is shewn as acting from *faith* and she is told that her faith has saved her and that her sins are cancelled. She acted, not from self-love, but from love.

To act from faith is not to act from self-love and its merits, its inevitable sense of being superior, of being better than others. This is the general meaning of the parable, although every incident in it has its own meaning.

To *act* from faith is to act from *beyond oneself*—to act beyond self-love and its interests. It is just the same in the case of thinking from faith. To think from the knowledge and ideas of faith is to think from *beyond* one's ordinary mind, *beyond* all ordinary ideas and ways of thought. To think from faith is to think in a new way: to act from faith is to act in a new way.

In all the parables about *faith* in the Gospels, the emphasis is laid on the fact that the approach to Christ—that is, the approach to the teaching about re-birth and the evolution of oneself—is impossible by visible aids or by means of the ordinary worldly thoughts and emotions. An exertion, an effort, is needed beyond what anyone would think or do ordinarily. The order of Truth belonging to the category of "faith" has nothing to do with the order of truth belonging to the senses, which is provable by the senses. When Nicodemus beheld the miracles and believed simply because of the miracles, he was told in so many words that it was all useless. The visible miracles, indeed, stood in his way. They could not touch that level of mind that can only be awakened through faith and that *faith* only can awake. A man does not come to the stage of inner under-standing belonging to *faith* by means of anything outer, anything seen. To live by the seen is to live on one level of life: to live by faith is to begin to live on another. And this other level, which is eventually the re-birth of a man, once he attains it, is a definite thing, a real state, an actual possibility, to which all the ideas of faith and its Truth and knowledge can eventually lift a man. A higher level of man can only be reached through a class of knowledge and ideas that *must be kept alive by continual effort*, and does not correspond to anything that life confirms. A man must look away from the scene of life to reach its meaning. Faith is thus a continual inner effort, a continual altering of the mind, of the habitual ways of thought, of the habitual ways of taking everything, of habitual reactions. To act from faith is to act from beyond the range of the ideas and reasons that the sense-known side of the world has built up in everyone's mind. On the side of love it is to *will* action beyond natural considerations, in the light of com-parison between *what one is* and what lies above one, what is possible. For its direction is to *another stage of a man* and so another level of himself to which life cannot raise him. So through having faith, a man's *attitude to life* will gradually change. He will see it no longer as the sole end. And he will no longer act always for the sake of the *man that he is* but for the New Man above himself, for the new possibility hidden in him.

In the above parable, or incident, the fact that Simon invited Christ to dine with him was nothing in itself. The approach to Christ was not through anything like that. The fact that Christ was at Simon's table, "visible" to him, was not the means of approach. The approach to Christ could only be through *faith*, not through the seen. It could only be *internal*. People imagine that getting into contact means chiefly to be visibly in contact, through the senses, and even think they can understand whatever they hear, even were they Christ's words, merely by hearing them spoken. But all that Christ represented could only be approached internally, by faith.

Simon is a portrait of a critical man, a man who might understand a little, but fears to do so, and is rude in consequence, out of a kind of nervousness. It is obvious that Simon thought it was kind of him to ask Christ to dine. He took a certain social risk in doing so. But he did not even bother to greet Christ politely or to do the customary things. And he wanted to point out what he regarded as Christ's shortcomings and criticise them. Yet he answered Christ civilly when asked a question. He understood a little, but could not behave rightly and wanted to find fault. Yet Christ dined with him. This means that this *type of man* is not incapable of understanding though his valuation is slight. "He loved little." Many definite ever-recurring *types* of men and women are drawn in the Gospels, with reference to their attitudes and their possibilities of understanding.

For example, three types of women are described in the Gospels—Mary, Martha and Mary Magdalene (that is, Mary, who came from Magdala). Mary Magdalene may have been the woman here who loved much and so was forgiven and told that her faith had saved her. What is the connexion between love and faith? The knowledge that is a matter of faith cannot enter the will unless there is love for it. It is not only a *change of mind* that connects a man with what is higher than himself, but a *change of will*—that is, a change of love, of what one loves. To love only oneself can lead nowhere. Love is of many kinds, just as knowledge is of many different kinds. Each kind of knowledge needs its own kind of love to bear any fruit.

The teaching of Christ represents a certain order of knowledge which in its turn requires a certain kind of love. The approach to Christ's teaching was only through *faith*. It could not be approached in any other way. His teaching could not be taken in the same way as ordinary teaching. To take the teaching of Christ on the same level as the sort of teaching that can be got at a school or college is to make it useless. Its order of knowledge could only be received in terms of *faith*. So Christ is constantly represented as looking for *signs of faith* in people— that is, for those qualities of understanding that belong to faith, which was the first thing necessary. He was looking for a quality in people that corresponded to faith—not a literal level of mind, not a self-love, but a level that could receive the teaching and grasp its meaning. And very few people were found who could understand a single thing of all that was being taught. They could neither "hear" nor "see" what was meant. They wanted to take everything in their own way and according to their own interests and to understand it in the same terms as they understood everything else in their daily life. They could not discriminate. They wanted to drag Christ's teaching about the transformation of Man down to their own level of thought, as Nicodemus did.

But a few are mentioned who had the quality of love for this order of teaching, without any knowledge of it. The woman at Christ's feet in Simon's house had love of this kind. Her love was discriminative. Through the quality of her love she could recognise the significance of Christ and through that could make contact. She is depicted as touching Christ's feet. Her approach began there, but it was already *faith*, and not physical. The feet of Christ touched the earth of her own self and she recognised the lower and higher in herself. So her approach to Christ was from *faith*, not from the knowledge that demands faith, but from the love that is necessary for that knowledge to grow, as a seed. That there was something rare in the quality of her love is represented not only by the alabaster box of ointment, but by the fact that she was forgiven. She was given the authority that her past was cancelled and so she could begin again. For no one can begin again otherwise.

What is the nature of this level of development to which faith leads? What is this evolution of a man, latent in him, about which the Gospels are always speaking? In order to understand something of what it means we must look at the parables about the *Kingdom of Heaven*.

Chapter Eleven

THE KINGDOM OF HEAVEN

PART ONE

ALTHOUGH no one can understand the level of life belonging to the *Kingdom of Heaven*, a man can understand the level of life on which he is. Everyone can see the nature of life in this world. He can see through his outer senses what is done by people on this level of life: and he can, if he looks at himself, see with his inner senses what he does. He will then see what life is like and what he is like at this level. And neither life nor himself can be different *at this level*. For, understood internally, the Universe is a series of levels, and a thing is what it is according to where it is, in this series. The level above Man is called the Kingdom of Heaven or Kingdom of God in the Gospels. It has many other names in different writings. In the Gospels, it is said that the Kingdom of Heaven is *within*. It is at a higher level of a man. To reach it a man must reach a higher level in himself. If everyone did this, the level of life on this earth would change. The whole earth would take a step up in evolution. But this step can only be taken by an individual man. A man can reach a higher level in himself and yet live in the life of this earth. Each person has an inner but different access to a higher level. It is a possibility in him, for Man is created as a being capable of a further individual evolution or, as it is called in the Gospels, a re-birth. A man does not have to wait until he observes with his very eyes a visible kingdom called the Kingdom of Heaven surrounding him. Christ said that the Kingdom of Heaven is not to be looked for as coming in a way that can be observed outwardly. He said: "And being asked by the Pharisees when the Kingdom of God cometh, he answereth them and said, The Kingdom of God cometh not with observation: neither shall they say, Lo, here! or, There! for lo, the Kingdom of God is within you" (Luke xvii, 20). The Kingdom of Heaven is an inner *state*, not an outer place. It is an inner state of development that a man can reach. There is no question of time and space, of *when* or *where* connected with it, for

124

it is above a man, always, as a higher possibility of himself. But we must understand that between these two levels often called "earth" and "heaven" are many
intermediate degrees. There are degrees of "earth", the highest of which is less
than the lowest degree of "heaven". For example, John the Baptist, who played
the part of herald to Christ's teaching, was not an ordinary man. He had received
teaching. He collected disciples round him, who, we are told, practised fasting.
But he had not attained the *lowest* level of the Kingdom of Heaven. Christ expressly says of him that the least in the Kingdom of Heaven was greater than he:
"Among them that are born of women there is none greater than John: yet he
that is but little in the Kingdom of God is greater than he" (Luke vii, 28).

John the Baptist had a very difficult part to play in the drama of Christ. He
had to preach the coming of Christ. He did not know Christ when he came to
him to undergo the formal rite of Baptism. And when John was reluctant
to baptise him, saying: "I have need to be baptised of thee, and comest thou to
me?" Christ said to him: "Suffer it now: for thus it becometh us to fulfil all
righteousness." He reminds John that he must play his part. Then John baptised
Christ. Afterwards John the Baptist said of Christ: "He must increase, but I
must decrease. He that cometh from above is above all: he that is of the earth
is of the earth, and of the earth he speaketh: he that cometh from heaven is above
all" (John iii, 30, 31). Later John the Baptist was beheaded at the request of the
daughter of Herodias, prompted by her mother, whose marriage with Herod,
her husband's brother, John had condemned from a legal point of view. It is
clear that John the Baptist knew what would take place. All this can only be
understood in terms of an *eventual* stage that could be reached by John, by his
deliberate undertaking of this difficult part, which, in a physical sense at least,
was as painful as that played by Jesus.

It is therefore clear that John the Baptist was instructed to play a definite part.
He knew Christ was to come and he recognised him by a certain sign, unseen
by others. And he actually speaks of someone who sent him to play the part
he had to fulfil. He says: "I knew him not (he is referring to Christ when he
first set eyes on him) but *he that sent me* to baptise with water, he said unto me,
Upon whomsoever thou shalt see the Spirit descending, and abiding upon him,
the same is he that baptiseth with the Holy Spirit." Who sent John? We are
not told. Christ refers to John the Baptist as a man born of woman—that is,

he had not undergone the re-birth taught by Christ. So he was still "of the earth". He belonged to the level called "earth", to the highest degree of it, but not to the lowest degree of the Kingdom of Heaven. He baptised with water—that is, Truth—and so he taught *repentance*, namely, *change of mind*, which is the real meaning of the word in the Greek, through the reception of knowledge or truth. The water was a representation of this. Baptism means cleansing. By "Truth" about a higher level the mind is cleansed of illusions belonging to the senses and to self-love. John the Baptist taught a knowledge, a Truth, that if accepted could cleanse the mind and lead a man to a change in thinking—that is, to "repentance" or "change of mind". He expressly says: "I am not the Christ. I am sent before him." And he says himself that he is not re-born, but still of the earth-level, but that Christ is above this level. Of Christ he says: "He that cometh from above is above all" and of himself he says: "He that is of the earth is of the earth, and of the earth he speaketh." And he adds, referring again to Christ: "He that cometh from heaven is above all." In all this, the two levels of "earth" and "heaven" are made distinct. But more than this is made distinct. There are degrees of "earth" and degrees of "heaven". For in speaking of the earth-level, Christ says of John the Baptist: "Among those that are born of women, there is none greater than he." That is, littleness and greatness belong to the earth-level of development as well as to the higher level. But even more is made distinct by these words of Christ. What is greatest on the level of earth does not pass *directly* into what is least on the level of the Kingdom of Heaven. To pass from the highest stage on the lower level to the lowest stage on the higher level demands a *re-birth* or transformation of a man. Christ taught repentance *and re-birth* and the Kingdom of Heaven. John the Baptist taught repentance and the idea of the Kingdom of Heaven, but he says nothing of re-birth. He had not been born "from above". The influences belonging to this higher level, called the Kingdom of Heaven, did not yet reach him. He was not "born of the Spirit". His inner state is further described, in the ancient language of parables, which speaks psychologically in terms of physical objects, by references to what he ate and what he was clothed in and what encircled him. He ate *wild* honey. He was clad in *skins* and girt with a *leather belt*. A man's clothing represents his attitudes—what he wears psychologically, what Truth his mind is clothed with. His girdle represents what binds him together, psychologically. His food represents what ideas he nourishes himself by. John feeds on wild honey and locusts. Locusts *devour*. They devour all growing life. Something very interesting is meant here. John the Baptist admits he is "of the earth". He can understand only from the earth-level. That is, whatever new teaching he had received, he saw from the "earth-level" or natural level of his mind. He understood the *new* in terms of the *old*.

Christ says in a parable, *in direct reference* to John and his disciples:

"No man rendeth a piece from a new garment and putteth it upon an old garment; else he will rend the new, and also the piece from the new will not agree with the old. And no man putteth new wine into old wine-skins; else the new wine will burst the skins, and itself will be spilled, and the skins will perish. But new wine must be put into fresh skins. And no man having drunk old wine desireth new: for he saith, The old is good." (Luke v, 36, 39.)

To receive new teaching aright, a man cannot take it in with all the prejudices, attitudes, racial or personal, all the viewpoints and illusions of the senses that life has formed in him. He cannot receive the new wine of the teaching in old bottles. The higher level cannot be received by the lower—the level of earth. Nor can the new teaching be merely *added* on to the old. It cannot be sewn on to the old. "No man rendeth a piece from a new garment and putteth it upon an old garment else he will rend the new." By taking one thing from the new and adding to the old, he will injure the new. The new garment means the new teaching, which, as it were, a man must put on and wear. The new must be accepted in its entirety, not tacked on to the old viewpoints. And again, not only will the new be rended, but, Christ says: "And also the piece from the new will not agree with the old." All this is said in reference to John the Baptist and his level of understanding by Christ after the Pharisees had taken an unfavourable view of Christ's disciples in comparison with John's. They said that John's disciples fasted and made supplications but Christ's disciples ate and drank.

PART TWO

BEFORE we begin to study the many parables used by Christ in his description of the higher level of development called the Kingdom of Heaven, let us take the phrase: "The Kingdom of Heaven is within you", and try to understand the word *within*. The "Kingdom of Heaven" is the highest state of evolution attainable by Man. To reach a new state of himself a man must change internally. He must become a New Man. A state is internal. The Kingdom of Heaven is internal. It is a state that can be reached by a man internally, through inner change. Can it be reached without inner change? A change of inner state may be brought about artificially, but this is not inner evolution. What a man must observe in himself, in what way he must think, what he must begin to value and aim at and so on, are constantly being taught by Christ as the means of inner evolution, up to that higher level called the Kingdom of Heaven. The *higher* level is *within* a man. Whether we say higher or more internal is the same thing, provided we understand that a higher state of a man exists potentially within him, just as does a more internal state. A man can be better than he is. This better state is *inner* or *higher* in regard to his present state. The Kingdom of Heaven, the highest state of a man, is thus internal to a man—that is, *within* the man he is; or it is at a higher level—that is, *above* the man he is. The idea is the same. Now a man of the senses, a sensual man, a literal man, a man of the *earth*, is an externally-minded man. The Kingdom of Heaven is not in that. As we have seen, John speaks of himself as being of the earth, while he speaks of Christ as coming "from above"; when John tells his disciples that Christ must increase while he himself must decrease, he goes on to say: "He that cometh *from above* is above all: he that is of the earth is of the earth, and of the earth he speaketh: he that cometh from heaven is above all" (John iii, 31). And in another place Christ explains to Nicodemus that a man must be born "from above". He says: "Verily, verily, I say unto thee, Except a man be born *from above*, he cannot see the Kingdom of God" (John iii, 3). "From above" might be rendered equally as "internally". A man must be born *internally*—internal to what he is. The Kingdom of Heaven is internal—*within you*—and it is also *above you*. Above and within are, psychologically, the same—that is, in the Gospels, *the internal is higher*: to put it another way, to reach a higher level of himself a man must go in an *internal direction*—into himself—so higher is internal and lower is external. Understand that a lower level is external and lies in the external man and a higher level is internal and lies in the internal man.

In the light of the idea that the Kingdom of Heaven is *within* a man, let us now try to see why Christ attacked the Pharisees so mercilessly, and from this realise what the Pharisee means, in regard to the possibility of inner evolution. To evolve a man must move *inwardly*. He must, to begin with, get behind himself and see what he is doing. We have grasped that to move in an inner direction is to move towards a higher level. Now we can understand something of the meaning and nature of moving inwards towards the Kingdom of Heaven which is within, if we realise what stands in the way. What can prevent a man from moving inwards? Many things can prevent him, but one of the chief things is the *Pharisee* in him, which cannot move inwards without dying, for it is in the external side of a man and loves applause. The Pharisees could not understand anything in their religion save in an external way. Their worship took a literal, external form and was not from the heart. Good is internal to Truth because it is higher than Truth. And so Truth, *understood* aright, should lead into the internal man. But Truth practised as an outer virtue cannot do so. Christ often told the Pharisees that they had no self-knowledge, no insight—that is, no internal understanding. He lashed them because they did everything in an external way for the sake of appearances and ruined men's minds with the greatest zeal. Christ uses very strong language about this external worship which prevents a man from entering the Kingdom of Heaven because it keeps him in externals, in the external side of himself, and also about this proselytising zeal which ruins people's minds, in so far as all future inner development is concerned. He says:

"But woe unto you, scribes and Pharisees, hypocrites! because ye shut the kingdom of heaven against men: for ye enter not in yourselves, neither suffer ye them that are entering in to enter. Woe unto you, scribes and Pharisees, hypocrites! for ye compass sea and land to make one proselyte; and when he is become so, ye make him twofold more a son of hell than yourselves."

(Matt. xxiii, 13, 15.)

You will notice here that Christ says directly that the Pharisees do not enter, but prevent others from entering, the Kingdom of Heaven. Why do they shut the Kingdom of Heaven against men? Since the Kingdom of Heaven is within a man and so is approached by a deeper understanding and through the development of his internal mind, the Pharisee in him shuts the Kingdom against him because it lays stress only on outer ritual and literal obedience—that is, on the external mind. As long as a man kept to the letter of the law, nothing ever mattered to the Pharisees as a class. They believed, for instance, that it was binding to swear by the gold of the temple but not by the temple. "Ye blind guides", Christ says of them, "who say whosoever shall swear by the temple, it is nothing, but whosoever shall swear by the gold of the temple, he is a debtor. Ye fools and blind: For which is greater, the gold or the temple that sanctifieth the gold?" (Matt. xxiii, 16–17.) The Pharisees took everything the wrong way round. They thought Man was made for the Sabbath and not that the Sabbath was made for Man. The spiritual meaning of the temple should have been far greater to them than the literal value of the visible gold in it. And it was just because they laid stress on the outer side of things and none on the inner, that they, as a class, shut the Kingdom of Heaven against men, and did not enter themselves or suffer others to do so. The psychological reason is plain. A man who lives in external meanings and in the literal things of the senses does not and cannot move internally in himself to deeper and infinitely finer meanings and so to new experiences in meaning. He fixes himself in the most external side of himself, which is the same as the lowest most sense-based side, and there he only feels and understands in a certain way. But the Kingdom of Heaven is *within* a man. It lies in the direction of his reflections and new under-standings and new thoughts. It is not on this external or lowest level in Man but internal to it and so above it. It is not difficult to see something of what is meant. Christ attacked the Pharisees because they stood at the opposite pole of under-standing from him. Christ represents in the Gospels the most evolved, the highest man. The Pharisee represents the man who cannot evolve because he is turned the wrong way round and gets everything upside down. The Pharisee is in externals, in merit, and in the love of external appearances. All this means, psychologically, that the *Pharisee in a man* cuts him off from entry into the Kingdom and prevents anything else in him from entering. All that you do to be seen of men, and for no other reason, is the Pharisee in you: he belongs to the external man in you. The "Pharisee" in Christ's references represented not only the most external hair-splitting religious beliefs but something much worse. Christ says much of their vanity and self-conceit and self-justifying but he speaks most strongly of all about their sin of *hypocrisy* which, he said, damned them. They did everything externally for appearance' sake and believe nothing internally. So they had no access *to what is internal in themselves*: and so they damned themselves. Thus they were their own punishment. It was of them that he spoke when he defined the sin against the

Holy Spirit. Are we then to understand that all this was the case with John the Baptist, who is said not to have reached even the lowest level of the Kingdom of Heaven? Obviously it would be impossible to do so. John was in the external and literal side of religious truth but, unlike the Pharisees, he was a genuine and sincere man. He is the herald of good tidings. He represents a stage of a man moving towards the inner kingdom, but still outside it, still seeing it from the level of the earth. He represents a stage in understanding. At such an inner stage the "old" and the "new" come into collision. We can realise that there must be a period when the old understanding may devour or destroy the new understanding. We noticed how the parables about new wine in old bottles and about a new patch on an old garment were spoken by Christ immediately after the Pharisees had contrasted Christ's disciples, whom they blamed for not fasting, with John the Baptist's disciples, who fasted. That John's understanding was still in external things and literal meaning is shewn in the description of his clothing. Christ connects him with Elias or Elijah. One reason is that John and Elijah represented similar stages of understanding the Truth of the Word of God. Elijah is said to have been clothed in hairy garments: John the Baptist wore camel's hair and a leather girdle. In II Kings (i, 8) the prophet Elijah is described in these words: "He was a man with a garment of hair and with a girdle of leather round his loins." And John the Baptist is described in Matthew (iii, 4) as follows: "Now John himself had his raiment of camel's hair and a leather girdle about his loins." In the ancient language of parables what a man is clothed in represents what his mind wears. A man's mind is clothed in what he holds as Truth, whether it be mere opinion, or deeper belief. So Truth is a garment of the mind and according to what the man holds as Truth so is the nature of the garment. Truth can be understood externally or internally. The Truth taught by Christ, called the Word of God, which is about inner evolution, can be understood in its external, literal meaning or in its deeper, internal meaning. If it is understood externally, then it is represented as a garment *made from external things*. Hair and leather are external things. They belong to the skin—to what is most external. Since the descriptions of the garments of Elijah and John the Baptist are similar, it means in the hidden language of parables that they were in a similar state in regard to their understanding of Truth. It was an external understanding, not an internal one. What held it together, the girdle, was of leather. That is, it was held together by something external, not internal. For example, when a man's beliefs depend on the behaviour of some one else, they are held together by external means. Or again, many people would not believe the teaching of Christ if the historical details were proved sufficiently inaccurate. Their belief is held together by something external. They do not yet see the *Good* of the Truth they have been taught. John the Baptist did not understand Christ in his method of teaching. Christ taught from Good. John remained uncertain about him. When John was in prison he sent to ask if Christ were really the Christ: "Art thou he that cometh or do we look for another?" Now if we compare what is said of the garment worn by Christ with what is said of John's garment, we can see that Christ was clothed in Truth in a quite different way from the manner in which John was clothed. When the soldiers who had crucified Christ parted his garments, it is said that "the coat was without seam, woven from the top throughout" (John xix, 23). Notice it was woven *from the top*—that is, *from above*. We have seen that *from above* and *internal* mean the same. John was in external Truth, Christ in internal Truth. And when a man is in Truth alone, when he acts and judges all things from Truth, from doctrine, from rules, from literal meaning, he is harsh and often without mercy. If all men acted from Good primarily, no sect would persecute another sect who held a different view of what Truth is. It is *Good* that unites Truth together into a living whole. It is *Good* that weaves together all the separate elements of the Truths that have led to it and softens them and brings them into a harmonious relation. John was in the harshness of doctrinal Truth, of Truth that had not yet fully led to what is properly the culmination of all Truth—namely, a new realisation of Good, a new *level* of Good. That is why Christ said of him that he was not clad in soft raiment which belongs to those in the Kingdom. His raiment was harsh—camel's hair and leather. So Christ said, speaking of John: "What went ye out for to see? a man clothed in soft raiment? Behold, they that wear soft raiment are in kings' houses" (Matt. xi, 8).

John the Baptist represents the side of Truth—that is, the law, without its *grace*. Christ is the union of Truth with Good. Good is above Truth. All Truth must lead to good. But, as we have seen elsewhere, Truth must come first and Good second, until Truth unites with its Good. Then Good comes first and Truth second. So, in the Gospel according to St John (who was not John the Baptist) it is written in the first chapter: "John (the Baptist) cried, 'This is He of whom I said "He who is coming after me has taken precedence of me for He existed before me." ' " Good is prior to Truth—to the law. Since God is good, Good is *prior* to all Truth—all law. And so St John adds: "The law was given through Moses: but grace and truth came through Jesus Christ." Grace, charity or Good has united with Truth in Jesus Christ. So St John says that Christ was in the *fulness*—that is, in the fulfilment of Truth which is Good—and so full of *grace* and Truth. And these early words in St John give the key to this Gospel, which is written in a different way from the first three Gospels and creates a different feeling. For it is written from grace, from Good, the emotional feeling of what Christ stood for in the world, and not from the side of Truth devoid of grace, from the letter, from the literal fact. In consequence, the whole Gospel produces a different impression of Christ's teaching and falls upon a different part of the understanding.

PART THREE

WHEN the conception of the Kingdom of Heaven begins to be grasped, a new and startling meaning of life dawns in the mind. The first parable given by Christ is that of the Sower. It is about the Kingdom of Heaven. Christ says of it that it is the parable of parables and unless it is understood other parables cannot be. You must realise that all the parables in the Gospels are about the Kingdom of Heaven and the parable of the Sower is the first. It is the starting-point of Christ's teaching about the mystery of the Kingdom. In the thirteenth chapter of Matthew, Christ begins to speak in parables to the multitude. Why? Because he is beginning to speak of the Kingdom of God. His disciples ask why he has suddenly begun to use parables and he says: "Unto you it is given to know the mysteries of the Kingdom of Heaven, but to them it is not given. For whosoever hath to him shall be given, and he shall have abundance: but whosoever hath not, from him shall be taken away even that which he hath. Therefore speak I to them in parables; because seeing they see not, and hearing they hear not, neither do they understand" (Matt. xiii, 11–13).

What is the first mystery that he reveals about the Kingdom? In the parable of the Sower it can be seen that the first mystery is that *Man is sown on to the earth as material for the Kingdom of Heaven.* To call it the parable of the Sower and the Seed is misleading unless it is understood that Man is the seed. Actually, there is no mention of seed. In Matthew (xiii, 3, 4) it is said in the Greek: "Behold the sower went forth to sow and as he sowed *some* fell by the wayside." The word *seed* is added in the English translation, so that it reads: "Behold the sower went forth to sow and as he sowed some seeds fell by the wayside." What is really meant? What did the sower sow? He sowed *men*. This is the first startling idea, hidden in the parable. Men are sown on earth as material for the Kingdom of Heaven—some by the wayside, some on rocky ground, some among thorns and some on good soil. It is only those in the last class that are capable of undergoing that inner evolution that brings them to the level of the Kingdom. It is plain that *men* are meant, because in his private explanation of the parable to his disciples Christ says: "When anyone heareth the word of the kingdom, and understandeth it not, then cometh the evil one, and snatcheth away that which hath been sown in his heart. This is *he* that was sown by the wayside" (Matt. xiii, 19). And he goes on to speak of "*he* that was sown on rocky ground" and "*he* that was sown among thorns" and "*he* that was sown upon the good ground". In the light of the Kingdom of Heaven, then, humanity on earth is an *experiment in inner evolution*.

After giving the parable of the Sower and its interpretation, Christ goes on to speak of the Kingdom from another aspect. First he has given the idea of the Kingdom in terms of human beings sown on the earth. Next he speaks of the teaching that is sown *upon these human beings* that can cause them to awake and evolve.

"Another parable he set before them, saying, The kingdom of heaven is likened unto a man that sowed good seed in his field; but while men slept, his enemy came and sowed tares also among the wheat, and went away. But when the blade sprang up, and brought forth fruit, then appeared the tares also. And the servants of the householder came and said to him, Sir, didst thou not sow good seed in thy field? whence then hath it tares? And he said unto them, An enemy hath done this. And the servants say unto him, Wilt thou then that we go and gather them up? But he saith, Nay; lest haply while ye gather up the tares, ye root up the wheat with them. Let both grow together until the harvest: and in the time of the harvest I will say to the reapers, Gather up first the tares, and bind them in bundles to burn them: but gather the wheat into my barn."
(Matt. xiii, 24–30.)

This parable is about the Word of the Kingdom—that is, the teaching that has to be given on earth and to be received and understood and followed, by that part of humanity capable of evolving at any particular time. The good seed is the Word of the Kingdom. The field in which it is sown is humanity on earth. But something happens, inevitably, in such teaching, each time it is sown on the earth. It gets mixed with error, with things that "cause stumbling". In the Greek the word translated as *tares* refers to a plant which looks like wheat when it begins to grow— i.e. it cannot be distinguished at first from wheat. Why does this mixture of the true and the false take place? The reason is given in the phrase *while men slept* which in the original is more striking still—literally, *in the sleep of men*. "The kingdom of heaven is likened unto a man that sowed good seed in his field: but in the sleep of men, his enemy came and sowed tares also among the wheat" (Matt. xiii, 25). This cannot mean, of course, that on some particular night when people were asleep the devil came and sowed tares. Error inevitably creeps in and contaminates the original teaching, and this so inextricably that it cannot be separated from the Truth. The reason is that *men sleep*. They cannot keep awake to the full meaning of the teaching given them. Many things are said about being asleep and keeping awake in the Gospels. Often the disciples are described as being *asleep* and it is not literal, physical sleep that is meant. And there are many references to the necessity of being *awake* in order to understand the Word of the Kingdom. Christ often says: "Watch", which in the Greek means "Be awake". Christ says: "What I say unto you I say unto all, *Be awake* (trans. Watch)". Again, he says: "Be awake (trans. Watch) for you know not when the master of the house cometh, lest coming suddenly he find you sleeping" (Mark xiii, 35). This refers to a state of inner awareness or awakeness in the house of one's own being at a certain critical time. When a man is overpowered by the world of the senses, by life as it appears, by all the events and tasks and frictions of daily existence, the teaching about inner evolution and a higher level of Man fades from his mind and appears remote and unreal. The outer swallows up the inner. He is then *asleep*, in the sense of the Gospels; and what he understood when he was awake internally he loses sight of or mingles with other meanings. And so it is understandable that all teaching about a higher level can become altered. The parable of the Tares shews us that a contamination of right understanding by wrong understanding takes place from the very beginning of every occasion when the teaching of the higher Kingdom is sown upon any part of Mankind. As he is, *Man cannot keep awake* sufficiently to receive and transmit the teaching in its original purity. It becomes mingled with his own personal prejudices or he alters something that seems to contradict something else, or leaves out something that he can make no sense of. In these and many other ways many mistakes and errors grow up side by side with what is genuine and true. The wheat in the parable is the true, genuine form of the teaching and the tares are the errors that inevitably get mingled with it, because Man cannot remain continually awake to that order of Truth that comes from a higher level of meaning. So it is said that *in the sleep of men*, the enemy came and sowed tares among the wheat. Teaching, then, that it is necessary for Man to know and do in order to bring about his inner growth and completeness, whereby he can reach the level of meaning and understanding called the Kingdom of Heaven— such teaching cannot exist on earth in its original purity owing to the sleep of men. It inevitably becomes mixed with falsity.

Let us recapitulate: Man is sown upon the earth as material for a step in development. He is material for the Kingdom of Heaven. But certain difficulties arise. All are not sown in favourable places. Again, Man must have knowledge given him. Knowledge about how to reach this stage of development called the Kingdom must be sown also—not upon the earth itself, but upon the earth of men's minds. But new difficulties arise. Errors always creep into the teaching about inner evolution and about what a man must believe and think and do in order to reach a higher level of his own nature and understanding. These errors cannot be separated from the Truth without danger of hurting the latter. So the situation cannot be remedied *on the earth* but only at the *end of the world*. (But of this we will speak later.)

PART FOUR

WE have seen from the Parable of the Sower that Man is sown on the earth itself as material for the Kingdom of Heaven. Then we have seen from the second great parable, that of the Wheat and Tares, that the teaching of the Kingdom is sown on Man. First Man is sown on the earth. Then the teaching of inner evolution is sown on Man on the earth. But in relation to this second sowing, Man is himself "earth". A man himself is "earth" on which the teaching of a higher level is sown. Let us try to see this concept as clearly as possible. Heaven sows Man on earth. Man is then on earth, but all men are not in the same state as regards the Kingdom. Man, then, on earth, is now in turn *earth*—a psychological earth—in the case of those who *can* receive the teaching sown on earth, which the second great Parable of the Wheat and Tares is about.

After the two great initial parables, that of the Sower of Man, and that of the Sowing of the teaching about his evolution, there follow two short parables, the Parable of the Man and the Grain of Mustard Seed and the Parable of the Woman and the Leaven. These follow directly on the Parable of the Wheat and Tares. They are related as follows in Matthew:

"Another parable set he before them, saying, The kingdom of heaven is like unto a grain of mustard seed, which a man took, and sowed in his field: which indeed is less than all seeds; but when it is grown, it is greater than the herbs, and becometh a tree, so that the birds of heaven come and lodge in the branches thereof.

Another parable spake he unto them; The kingdom of heaven is like unto leaven, which a woman took, and hid in three measures of meal, till it was all leavened." (Matt. xiii, 31–33.)

What do these two parables mean? If you will think, you will see that they refer to the *taking* of the Word of the Kingdom. First we have been given the parable of the sowing of Man on earth itself and next the parable about the sowing or teaching on the "earth" of Man himself. So it is only to be expected that now there will follow parables about how Man, as "earth", receives or takes the teaching itself.

Notice first of all about these two brief parables that the idea of *taking* appears in both. Taking what? Taking hold of the teaching sown on Man. They are obviously parables about how Man can take hold of the teaching sown on him. To take is the first thing that is necessary. The man *takes* the seed—that is, he must take hold himself of the teaching of the Kingdom. More than this, to *take* implies that he puts forth his hand in order to take, and *hand* in the ancient language of parables is power, because, in a physical or literal sense, through his hand a man is able to take what he wishes. To *take*, then, means that the man thinks and chooses for himself: and so *from himself* takes hold of the teaching of the Kingdom of

THE NEW MAN

Heaven. In the first parable it is said that the man not only takes but *sows*. He takes and sows the "least of all seeds". Where does he sow it? He takes and sows it *in his field*. This means *in what is his own*. We have an external side which is not our own and an internal side which is ourselves. In Luke it says *in his own garden*. And when he has done all this, when the man has taken the seed himself and sown it in his own garden, the seed grows into a tree. In which direction does it grow? It reaches up from the level of his earthly mind to the level of higher mind called the Kingdom of Heaven. Then he begins to know what thought on a higher level means. Thoughts come to him, not of the earth, but of a subtlety and fulness and fineness of meaning far above the coarse nature of thought belonging to the sense-based earth mind. This is the true growth of meaning and so this is the mind in its real development by the branching of meaning as of a tree. The development of the mind is through perceiving finer and finer meanings. It develops by becoming aware of finer and finer distinctions. The *birds of heaven* come and lodge in the branches of this developing thought. Birds represent thoughts in the language of parables. Here, birds denote the finer meanings and thoughts that belong to the level of the Kingdom of Heaven. It is comparable with a person with bad eyesight who sees everything dimly receiving new and finer eyes.

* * *

Now let us try to find some meaning in the second parable. Notice that the images are different. Man, seed and ground are not used, but instead Woman, leaven and meal. But here it is said also that something is taken. The woman *takes* the leaven and *hides* it. She does not take and *sow* it. Why does she hide it? Christ speaks elsewhere of the *leaven of the Pharisees*. He warns his disciples about this leaven, saying, "Take heed and beware of the leaven of the Pharisees and Sadducees." They cannot understand him and think he is talking of literal leaven. He rebukes them for taking his words literally and thinking that he spoke of bread. "Then understood they how that he bade them not beware of the leaven of bread, *but of the teaching of the Pharisees and Sadducees*" (Matt. xvi, 12). Why was this leaven evil? Did the Pharisees *hide* anything? On the contrary, religion with them was all ostentation and despising. It was "to be seen of men". It was all outer merit, virtue, respectability. Christ called this *adultery*—mixing the true with the false. The woman hid the teaching of the Kingdom in her heart and worked secretly.

138

She needed no audience. She saw its *Good* and so the whole of her was affected. In the inner meaning, the number three denotes *whole*. So in the parable it is said that the woman hid the leaven in *three* measures of meal until the *whole* was leavened. *Three* and the *whole* are the same. If a person acts from the *will*, the whole is affected. The woman hid the leaven because by *taking* it she shewed that she valued it, as very precious. One does not speak of what is most precious. But it did not become an intellectual growth in her. It acted on her through her emotional valuation, her feeling, and so in a hidden way. The Kingdom of Heaven acted on her by her taking hold of its meaning and valuing it so much that she hid it. She received it in her heart as what was good. The working of the heart is hidden. It acted on her *will*, not on her mind, as it acted on the mind of the man in the other parable. It was the good of its teaching that she took, not the *Truth*, as did the man. These two ways of receiving the teaching of the Kingdom of Heaven are exemplified in the two Parables of the Mustard Seed and the Leaven—as the man who received it as Truth in the mind and the woman who received it in the heart as Good. They represent apart from Man and Woman two ways of receiving the teaching of the Kingdom of Heaven: one is mainly through thought and the other is mainly through feeling. It is in this way that these two lesser parables about *taking*, following upon the previous two great parables, can be given a meaning. And so it can be understood that these four parables form, as it were, a complete picture of the meaning of the Kingdom of Heaven in relation to Man on earth.

Let us now look at the interpretation of the Parable of the Wheat and the Tares given by Christ. It comes after the Parable of the Woman and the Leaven. In it Christ makes no reference to the *sleep of Man* through which the errors or *tares* are sown. He has already mentioned this in the explanation to his disciples of why he teaches the multitude in *parables* and not openly. The Parable of the Wheat and the Tares is narrated as follows:

"The kingdom of heaven is likened unto a man that sowed good seed in his field: but while men slept, his enemy came and sowed tares also among the wheat, and went away. But when the blade sprang up, and brought forth fruit, then appeared the tares also. And the servants of the householder came and said unto him, Sir, didst thou not sow good seed in thy field? whence then hath it tares? And he said unto them, An enemy hath done this. And the servants say

unto him, Wilt thou then that we go and gather them up? But he saith, Nay;
lest haply while ye gather up the tares, ye root up the wheat with them. Let
both grow together until the harvest: and in the time of the harvest I will say
to the reapers, Gather up first the tares, and bind them in bundles to burn them:
but gather the wheat into my barn.'' (Matt. xiii, 24–30.)

The interpretation of this parable is as follows:

"He that soweth the good seed is the Son of Man; and the field is the world;
and the good seed, these are the sons of the kingdom; and the tares are the sons
of the evil one; and the enemy that sowed them is the devil; and the harvest
is the end of the world; and the reapers are the angels. As therefore the tares
are gathered up and burned with fire; so shall it be in the end of the world.
The Son of Man shall send forth his angels, and they shall gather out of his
kingdom all things that cause stumbling, and them that do iniquity, and shall
cast them into the furnace of fire: there shall be the weeping and gnashing of
teeth. Then shall the righteous shine forth as the sun in the kingdom of their
Father.'' (Matt. xiii, 37–43.)

The explanation of the meaning of *tares* is made clear. It is, first of all, all errors,
all things that cause stumbling, in connexion with the teaching of the Kingdom
or higher level of the development of Man; and second, it is all those who act
wrongly within the teaching. The tares are the seed of the evil one, because they
represent both the wrong teaching itself and the wrong results arising from it
(owing to the sleep of Man). The same applies to the seed of the Kingdom, or the
wheat, which is both the true teaching itself and the results of it acting on those
who are planted on the good soil. The phrase translated as "end of the world"
means "consummation of the age". The destruction of the material earth is not
meant. So far we have seen, in our attempt to understand something about the
Kingdom of Heaven and the teaching concerning it, that men are sown on the
earth differently, that they form the material for the Kingdom, that the true teaching about the Kingdom and how to reach it, which in its turn is sown upon men's
minds, becomes mingled with false views owing to the *sleep of Man*, and this so
inextricably that a separation cannot be made until the "end of the world"—that
is, until the "consummation of the age". What does an *age* mean? An age is a period

of time characterised by a particular teaching about inner evolution or the level of the Kingdom of Heaven. It comes to an end and a new form of the same teaching is then sown, adjusted to the prevalent conditions. A new harvest appears but always mingled with tares. A new reaping and a new separation is made, and the process is again repeated. Each form of the teaching about the Kingdom, from its inception to its culmination, is an *age*. Each action of the teaching is a *selective* action. Those who have, in any particular age, received the teaching about inner evolution and have followed it, thirty-, sixty- or one hundred-fold, are the harvest; and they attain "eternal" life on the level of the Kingdom of Heaven. In this connexion we must remind ourselves of Christ's words: "In my father's house are many mansions" (John xiv, 2).

PART FIVE—THE IDEA OF SELECTION

In the teaching about the Kingdom of Heaven and its relation to humanity on earth as given in the thirteenth chapter of Matthew, three further parables follow upon the four great introductory parables which we have studied. These three parables refer to the idea of *selection*. One of them is as follows:

"Again the kingdom of heaven is like unto a net, that was cast into the sea, and gathered of every kind: which, when it was filled, they drew up on the beach; and they sat down, and gathered the good into vessels, but the bad they cast away. So shall it be in the end of the world; the angels shall come forth and sever the wicked from among the righteous, and shall cast them into the furnace of fire: there shall be the weeping and gnashing of teeth."

(Matt. xiii, 47–50.)

Let us consider this parable in connexion with those thoughts that arise in the mind about *unfairness* or *injustice*. Everything that is said about the higher level of the Kingdom, from the very first parable about it, seems *unjust*. It is quite clear that the Kingdom of Heaven is not attainable by everyone in any one particular cycle of time. It is also clear from other parables about it, such as that of the marriage feast to which those invited did not come, that of those who can reach it few make the attempt. But let us first consider the Parable of the Net and the separation of the good and bad caught by it. Here the idea of selection is obvious. The good are gathered into vessels and the bad cast away. The same idea of the separation of the good from the bad appears in the Parable of the Tares. Is the idea of *selection* really unjust? Is it not *justice*? And is it not true that in ordinary life, *selection* plays a major part? Are not people selected for their particular jobs? People accept the idea of selection by examinations, and so on, and do not regard it as unjust if some pass and others fail. They even accept the theoretical idea of *natural selection* by the survival of the fittest and do not regard it as unjust. One thing eats another: weeds fight with plants. Nor do you expect all the seeds you sow in the ground to come up. You do not think it unfair if they do not. Wherever life exists there is a struggle. People vary very much in their capacities. In every form of human society, selection is at work. Some are good at one thing, some at another. In every department of human skill, some will be best and some will be worst, and a selection of the best must be made. All human education is based on the principle of the selection of the best. One does not expect, say, a school of engineering to select the worst students and send them out into the world as capable engineers. Such a proceeding would be not merely meaningless, but definitely *unjust*. For a thing to be in a place where it does not belong is unjust. You cannot, in short, separate the meaning of *justice* from that of *selection* if you come to think of it.

The other two parables are again about selection, but they refer to *inner selection*. And here we must notice that the idea of buying and selling is used. Buying means, to begin with, on this personal level, *taking*, and selling means *getting rid of*.

"The kingdom of heaven is like unto a treasure hidden in the field; which a man found, and hid; and in his joy he goeth and selleth all that he hath, and buyeth that field.

Again, the kingdom of heaven is like unto a man that is a merchant seeking goodly pearls: and having found one pearl of great price, he went and sold all that he had, and bought it." (Matt. xiii, 44–46.)

These two parables are about the *individual*. They are about what an individual man must do internally, in himself, to gain the level of the Kingdom of Heaven. He must become a good merchant and know what to buy and what to sell. Now what is it especially that a man must get rid of—must sell before he can buy? In

Luke (xviii, 22) it is related that when the rich prince (the Greek word here means prince, not ruler) asked Christ what he should do to inherit eternal life—that is, to reach the Kingdom of Heaven or the level of fully-developed Man—Christ said to him: "Sell all that thou hast." And in another place in the same Gospel (Luke xii, 33) Christ says, in general: "Sell that ye have." What must be sold? What must be got rid of? In the second instance given above, Christ tells his disciples one thing that they must get rid of and that is anxiety. He tells them that they can do nothing by being anxious which means literally in the Greek "having a divided mind". He says: "And which of you by being anxious can add a cubit to his stature? If then ye are not able to do even that which is least, why are ye anxious concerning the rest? . . . Howbeit seek ye the Kingdom of God and these things shall be added unto you" (these things about which ye are anxious) (Luke xii, 25, 26, 31). Here we see one thing that a man must *sell* in order to buy the pearl or the treasure. He must sell, that is, get rid of, certain sides of himself, and by selling these sides, he can gain enough to buy *what he values most*. The idea that is expressed in these two parables cannot be clear unless it is understood that in order to evolve to the level of the Kingdom of Heaven a man must first of all get rid of certain things in him. He must sell them, which means here that he must ultimately get rid of them. Only in this way can he make room for what is new, and only in this way can he gain the means to *buy*—that is, to take to himself as his own. So, by means of getting rid of many wrong ideas, many wrong ways of thinking and feeling, many useless anxieties, etc., by selling them, a man is in a position to buy what he really values. He cannot buy anything new unless, first of all, he sells, and through selling he gets the "money" to buy. In the two parables quoted, the merchant and the men who found the treasure are both represented as selling all that they had in order to buy that which they really valued.

PART SIX

THE final parable of the seven introductory parables about the meaning of the Kingdom of Heaven given in the thirteenth chapter of Matthew is that of the net cast into the sea which gathered of every kind, out of which the good were separated from the bad. Christ then asks his disciples if they have understood everything taught them in these seven parables about the Kingdom of Heaven and its relation to Man on Earth. To our astonishment the disciples answer that they have. In the narrative it is put in this way: after finishing his interpretation of the net let down into the sea, Christ says to his disciples: "Have ye understood *all these things*?" They say unto him: "Yea." The answer is extraordinary. How could they possibly understand *all these things*?

What man can possibly understand *all* the mysteries of the Kingdom of Heaven, when it is so difficult to catch even a single glimpse of one of their meanings? And it must be remembered that it was especially difficult for the disciples to understand the Kingdom in any other sense than as a purely literal kingdom on earth that was eagerly awaited. They looked for a great king who would rule over the whole earth and exalt their nation to supreme power and destroy or enslave all other nations. This was the Jewish dream of the promised Messiah. How could they understand that the Kingdom of Heaven was of Truth and inner righteousness? How could they understand that it was attained by an inner change, by a development of a man's inner spirit, and that a man made himself fit to enter it, in this life and the next, by an evolution of the whole *psychic* man, that is, by an evolution of all his mind, his love, his will and his understanding? Out of these inner changes the *Man of the Kingdom* is born. This is what Christ taught. This is why he said a man must internally be re-born, before he can see the Kingdom. But the disciples thought that it was an earthly kingdom that he spoke of, and that they, by race, were already "men of the kingdom". They thought that Christ was going to be a great and terrible king on earth and that soon he would prove to be so. How then could they understand the meaning of the first seven parables given them by Christ about the mysteries of the Kingdom? How could it satisfy their earthly ambitions? Yet when asked by Christ whether they understood "all these things" they answer: "Yea." Do not imagine that Christ believed them. Notice what Christ goes on to say after they have given their affirmative answer. He says:

> "Therefore every scribe who hath been made a disciple to the kingdom of heaven is like unto a man that is a householder, which bringeth forth out of his treasure things new and old." (Matt. xiii, 52.)

In these words Christ shews them that they do not understand. It is because of their answer *Yea* that Christ says: "*Therefore* every scribe . . . etc." They have been told for the first time about the Kingdom of Heaven in its real and spiritual meaning and they think they understand, just as everyone thinks he can understand a thing once it is told him. But all that they had just heard about the kingdom was new to them. It had nothing to do with their earthly ambitions. The whole idea of the Kingdom, as taught them in these seven parables by Christ, was utterly new to them. How could they understand it all? It was on another level of meaning. It was not about a literal, external, earthly kingdom—a kingdom of the world. The Kingdom of Heaven was *within* them. It was *above* them, not literally in the sky, but above their present level of themselves, above the level of the kind of people they were—above them, as a step in their own individual possible evolution. But how could they understand this? How could they realise at once on the first hearing of it that the mystery of the Kingdom lies in inner self-evolution? Yet they answered: "Yea"—meaning "We understand." So Christ said: *"Therefore"*— that is, because of the answer you have given and because you do not understand —"therefore every such scribe who hath been made a disciple to the Kingdom of Heaven is like unto a man who is a householder, which bringeth forth out of his treasure (or stores) things new and old." Notice that the disciples of the Kingdom —that is, those who are learning about its meaning—are here called *householders*— and, in fact, all who are instructed in the mysteries of the Kingdom are called householders. That is, they who are instructed in the mysteries are, psychologically, *householders*. Yes—but notice what they do. As householders they mix up the *new* and the *old*. They do not understand the entirely new teaching but mingle it with the old views and attitudes and thoughts already stored in their minds. The word translated as "treasure" means literally *stores*. They bring forth the new and the old together from their stores. Here we can see a connexion with those parables about the *new* wine in old bottles and the new patch on an old garment, where Christ shewed so clearly that the *new* could not be mixed with the *old*.

"No man rendeth a piece from a new garment and putteth it upon an old garment; else he will rend the new, and also the piece from the new will not agree with the old. And no man putteth new wine into old wine-skins; else the new wine will burst the skins, and itself will be spilled, and the skins will perish. But new wine must be put into fresh skins." (Luke v, 36–39.)

If a man mixes the new with the old, the *new* loses its power in him. The old views, the old values, the old estimations and standpoints, based on everyday life, based on tradition, based on appearances, based on the sense-produced mind, destroys the *new* teaching. It takes force from the *new*, so that the new has no power in the presence of the old viewpoint. For this reason there is added, at the end of the thirteenth chapter of Matthew, the remarkable account of how Christ (who is the *new*) had no power among those who were of his own country and who saw him in the light of their old associations. And this account can only be understood in terms of Christ's remarks to his disciples. This is why it is put in at this place in the narrative. Those among whom he was born saw him by association, in the old way, as the son of a carpenter. So the narrative goes straight on to say, after his remark to his disciples about the householder mixing the new and the old:

"It came to pass, when Jesus had finished these parables, he departed thence. And coming into his country, he taught them in their synagogue, insomuch that they were astonished, and said, Whence hath this man this wisdom, and these mighty works? Is not this the carpenter's son? is not his mother called Mary? and his brethren, James, and Joseph, and Simon, and Judas? And his sisters, are they not all with us? Whence then hath this man all these things? And they were offended in him. But Jesus said unto them, A prophet is not without honour, save in his own country, and in his own house. And he did not many mighty works there because of their unbelief." (Matt. xiii, 53–58.)

Here it is plain that when Christ and all that he represented, which is the "new", met with the "old", the force of the new was rendered powerless. And so we can understand that this passage is an illustration of what Christ has said to his disciples; here he shows that *the old cannot receive the new*, in that he himself was unable to manifest his power amongst his old associations, amongst his family.

We have now given one line of meaning to all that is recorded in the thirteenth chapter of Matthew and we have seen that everything said in it falls together in a common framework of meaning. And finally we have seen that the answer "*Yea*" of the disciples believing that they understood already shows that they misunderstood and that once the seed of the Kingdom of Heaven is sown on Man it becomes changed from the start and is falsified by being mixed with old views and old ways of thought—and so tares are sown side by side with the wheat.

Chapter Twelve

JUDAS ISCARIOT

ONE of the strangest incidents in the Gospels is the betrayal of Christ by Judas Iscariot. As it stands, it is nearly inexplicable. Christ taught openly. Any one of the authorities, Jewish or Roman, who wished to arrest him, could have easily found out where he was. The more this incident and the things connected with it are studied the more does it seem obvious that it *represents* something, that it has behind it an inner meaning. In other words, Christ was betrayed by Judas in quite another sense than the literal one. It is clear that Judas represented a total under-valuation, a misunderstanding, and finally a betrayal of Christ's teaching. Addressing his disciples, Christ says: "Did I not choose you the twelve and one of you is a devil?" He is referring to Judas Iscariot. Yet notice that Christ *chose* Judas. "Did I not choose you the twelve, and one of you is a devil?" (John vi, 70.) Judas failed Christ and so did Simon Peter, but we must understand that the failure of Simon Peter represents something quite different from the failure of Judas Iscariot. But both of them *represent* something. Peter denied Christ *three* times—that is, eventually *fully*; and he is shewn by Christ as representing the Church. But Judas does not represent the Church that passed into the world and struggled century after century against the violence and bestiality of Man on earth and enabled culture to exist. The inner meaning of a teaching about the Kingdom of Heaven must eventually be gradually lost in external forms and rituals, in quarrels about words, and so on—that is, *Christ*, who is the inner and purest meaning of the teaching itself, must eventually be denied, in process of time. But every teaching of the higher level of evolution of Man is followed by a fresh one. The teaching comes again. Christ speaks of his second coming and asks: "When the Son of Man cometh, shall he find faith on earth?" (Luke xviii, 8.) The *three* denials made by Peter of Christ and the ultimate failure of faith on earth at the consummation of the age, foreseen in the above passage, are connected. But a thing is not judged by its terminal stage in time. It is the whole "age" that is the total life of a thing—the whole day, not the last hour

of darkness—not its last moments. The Church was established. It grew: and it did prevail against evil. Peter is not shewn as rejecting Christ, but as denying him once, then again, and finally for the third time (and so fully) at night, at the end of the day, or rather, just before another "day" begins, when the cock crows. But Judas Iscariot is represented as rejecting Christ entirely. He did not deny him but rejected him. He is made to appear as if he thought of Christ as an ordinary man, but innocent. It is recorded of him that when he "repented" he spoke of Christ as being innocent. This is shewn in Matthew where Judas is said to repent.
The passage runs thus:

> "Then Judas, which betrayed him, when he saw that he (Christ) was condemned, repented himself, and brought back the thirty pieces of silver to the chief priests and elders, saying, I have sinned in that I betrayed innocent blood. But they said, What is that to us? See thou to it. And he cast down the pieces of silver into the sanctuary, and departed; and he went away and hanged himself."
> (Matt. xxvii, 3–5.)

It is said here that Judas "repents himself". But the word used in the Greek has nothing to do with—μετάνοια the change of mind, or repentance, that Christ taught. It means merely "to be concerned about". Did Judas really think that he had sinned only because he had betrayed "innocent blood", or did he know who Christ was? If he knew, how could he act as he did? Was there some reason? Did one of the disciples have to *represent* the rejection of Christ by the Jews, and play this difficult part, as John the Baptist had to play his own difficult part of herald? We have seen that John the Baptist was *told*. He was given instructions. He says: "He that sent me *said unto me*, Upon whomsoever thou shalt see the Spirit descending, and abiding upon him, the same is he that baptiseth with the Holy Spirit" (John i, 33). Is there any indication that Judas was *told*—that he too received instructions? Yes, there are two passages that indicate that Judas was acting on instructions from Christ. In Matthew (xxvi) it is recorded that after Judas had kissed him as a signal for his arrest, Jesus said to him: "Friend, do that for which thou art come." And in John (xiii) Jesus' words to Judas at the Last Supper are significant as representing a command. The disciples had asked Christ which of them should betray him.

"Jesus therefore answereth, He it is, for whom I shall dip the sop, and give it him. So when he had dipped the sop, he taketh and giveth it to Judas, the son of Simon Iscariot. And after the sop, then entered Satan into him. Jesus therefore saith unto him, That thou doest, do quickly. . . . He then having received the sop went out straightway, and it was night."

(John xiii, 26–30.)

What was the sop, and what did it contain, so that it is expressly said: "After the sop, Satan entered into him"? Perhaps it contained some substance that made it possible for Judas to carry out what he had been ordered to do and which otherwise he could not have done. For Jesus says plainly that he must now act. He says: "*That thou doest, do quickly.*" And the account again emphasises the importance of the sop, for it adds: "He then having received the sop went out straightway, and it was night." It does not say that the sop was a signal to Judas. It shows rather that, after the sop, Judas had the power to do evil. A change came over him. And in his conversation with Pilate later on, Jesus says that Pilate would have had no power but for Judas: "Thou wouldest have no power against me, except it were given thee from above: therefore he that delivered me unto thee hath greater sin" (John xix, 11). Was Judas forced to act as he did, or did he act unconsciously, from the kind of man he was: or did he act consciously, and deliberately take upon him a part which had to be enacted? Of one thing we can be quite certain: Judas was fulfilling the Scriptures. In this respect at least he was playing a part. Often it is said in the Gospels that something was done in order that the Scriptures might be fulfilled. Christ himself is recorded as saying to his disciples: "all things must needs be fulfilled, which are written in the law of Moses, and the prophets, and the psalms, concerning me" (Luke xxiv, 44). Throughout the Gospels it is made clear that Christ was acting deliberately and that he chose his disciples, Judas as well as the rest, for the parts that they had to play in the great drama which was foreseen and arranged in every detail. The first figure in the arranged drama was John the Baptist who had already played his part. Christ told his disciples that he was to be crucified. It is related in John that when Andrew and Philip tell him that certain Greeks are come to see him, he accepts this as a sign that the time has come, and says: "The hour is come, that the Son of Man should be glorified" (John xii, 23). He draws the disciples apart and warns them that he must suffer death. He does not seek to avoid this fate, but says: *"For this cause came I unto this hour."* It is stressed that in all details the Scriptures must be fulfilled. When the soldiers come to arrest Jesus he rebukes Peter for attempting to stop them, saying: "Thinkest thou that I cannot beseech my Father, and he shall even now send me more than twelve legions of angels? How then should the scriptures be fulfilled that thus it must be? . . . All this is come to pass, that the scriptures of the prophets might be fulfilled."   (Matt. xxvi, 53–56.)

In this consciously enacted drama which had its own foreseen fulfilment, Judas Iscariot had the most difficult part of all to play. Let us consider how he fulfilled the Scriptures. After he had cast down the thirty pieces of silver in the sanctuary and had gone away to hang himself, it is said in Matthew:

"And the chief priests took the pieces of silver, and said, It is not lawful to put them into the treasury, since it is the price of blood. And they took counsel, and bought with them the potter's field, to bury strangers in. Wherefore that field was called, The field of blood, unto this day. Then was fulfilled that which was spoken by Jeremiah the prophet, saying, And they took the thirty pieces of silver, the price of him that was priced, whom certain of the children of Israel did price; and they gave them for the potter's field, as the Lord appointed me."   (Matt. xxvii, 6–9.)

It is clear, then, that Judas did what he did in fulfilment of the Scriptures. That is, he acted as he was meant to act. But did he act consciously or not?

Let us look at that part of ancient Scripture which he had to fulfil. It is not in Jeremiah, but in Zechariah. The prophet is describing how he is told by the Lord to feed a certain flock—that is, in this case, to teach certain of the Jewish people. He takes two rods or staves for this purpose—that is, he teaches them through two sources of power (for a rod represents power) one of which he calls Beauty or Graciousness and the other Bands or Bindings (or Union). They are the *Good* of the teaching and the *Truth* of it. He says:

"And I took unto me two staves; the one I called Beauty, and the other I called Bands; and I fed the flock. Three shepherds also I cut off in one month; and my soul loathed them, and their soul abhorred me. Then said I, I will not feed you: that that dieth, let it die; and that that is to be cut off, let it be cut off; and let the rest eat every one the flesh of another."

All this means that his teaching was not received. To die, here, means internal death which ensues when good is lost sight of. The prophet continues:

"And I took my staff, even Beauty, and cut it asunder, that I might break my covenant, which I had made with all the people. And it was broken in that day: and so the poor of the flock that waited upon me knew that it was the word of the Lord. And I said unto them, If ye think good, give me my price; and if not, forbear. So they weighed for my price thirty pieces of silver. (This means that they valued his teaching at very little.) And the Lord said unto me, Cast it unto the potter: a goodly price that I was prised at of them. And I took the thirty pieces of silver, and cast them to the potter in the house of the Lord. Then I cut asunder mine other staff, even Bands, that I might break the brotherhood between Judah and Israel."   (Zechariah xi, 7–14.)

The obvious connexion between this passage and the tragedy of Judas lies in the valuation of the prophet, and the valuation of Christ at thirty pieces of silver. That the teaching is meant, is shewn clearly in the above verses. The phrase, "And the Lord said, Cast it (the thirty pieces) unto the potter, the goodly price that I was prised at of them" is meant sarcastically—i.e. "the marvellous price that I was valued at." Judas had to act all this—to represent the failure of the teaching in its inner meaning. He had to represent with literal money that valuation of Christ and his teaching which in the verses of Zechariah was made by those who received a similar teaching from the prophet.

If Judas Iscariot was an evil man, why is it that the disciples say nothing against him? He had been chosen by Christ and was with him for something like three years—that is, through the *full* period of Christ's teaching. This has not an historical meaning, for *three* always had the meaning of completeness. None of the first three writers of the Gospels says anything against Judas. When Christ tells his disciples at the Last Supper that one of them will betray him, it is not recorded that any suspicion fell on Judas. In Mark it is said that one by one the disciples asked Christ: "Is it I?" In John it is said that "the disciples looked one on another, doubting of whom he spake." Even when Judas went out into the night after receiving the sop and hearing Christ's command, it is particularly stressed that "no man at the table knew for what intent he (Christ) spake this unto him." (John xiii, 28.) Nor is there any comment even here by the writer of the Gospel.

APPENDIX

The man without a wedding-garment reaches the Kingdom of Heaven. Yes, he goes *upstairs* and should not. By what means? By cleverly pretending. The parable is related in Matthew:

"The kingdom of heaven is likened unto a certain king, which made a marriage-feast for his son, and sent forth his servants to call them that were bidden to the marriage-feast; and they would not come. Again he sent forth other servants, saying, Tell them that are bidden, Behold, I have made ready my dinner: my oxen and fatlings are killed, and all things are ready: come to the marriage-feast. But they made light of it, and went their ways, one to his own farm, another to his merchandise: and the rest laid hold on his servants, and entreated them shamefully, and killed them. But the king was wroth; and he sent his armies, and destroyed those murderers, and burned their city. Then said he to his servants, The wedding is ready, but they that were bidden were not worthy. Go ye therefore unto the partings of the highways, and as many as ye shall find, bid to the marriage-feast. And those servants went out into the highways and gathered together all as many as they found, both bad and good, and the wedding was filled with guests. But when the king came in to behold the guests, he saw there a man which had not on a wedding-garment: and he saith unto him, Friend, how camest thou in hither not having a wedding-garment? And he was speechless. Then the king said to the servants. Bind him hand and foot, and cast him out into the outer darkness; there shall be the weeping and gnashing of teeth. For many are called, but few are chosen."

(Matt. xxii, 2–14.)

Who were the guests? Notice that those guests were found at the parting of the highways. One of them is without a wedding-garment. A man reaches a certain understanding. Up to a certain point he understands. Is he going to follow what he understands? He comes to the parting of the ways. He has taken in intellectually what he has been taught, because to reach the "parting of the ways" he must have received some teaching. He may have preached, swayed thousands

152

by his rhetoric. Did he believe internally what he taught externally? This man without a wedding-garment has no intention of believing in what he has said. No doubt he appears good, kind, long-suffering, charitable. He uses the right words. He deceives everyone. He can ape any of the virtues. But interiorly he believes nothing. It is all outer show. Coming into the strong light of those far more conscious than himself, he ceases to deceive. His inner lack of belief is seen. Internally he is naked. A wedding-garment signifies desire for union. To be wed is to unite with what is beyond you—not yourself. This can only come from the *inner* man in you. This man is all self and show and reputation. All he does is self. He loves no one but himself and so has no inner side. The highest in himself is himself. But he acts well. He is an actor—ὑποκριτής—a hypocrite. Outwardly, he seems to believe what he says. Inwardly he believes nothing. So, inwardly, he has no wedding-garment. He does not wish his being to wed with what he teaches. Coming to those whose vision can penetrate outer pretence, he clearly has no wedding-garment. He has no desire to unite with what he teaches. Why? Because he has nothing of goodness in him. Even if what he teaches is Truth, he will not marry it.